Trying to Reinvent Your Career After 50?
Hoping to Find the Answer?
Why Settle for Just One?

There is no one right path to HOW TO FIND A JOB AFTER 50. In these pages you'll be introduced to a wide range of creative solutions that have worked for other mature job seekers from all walks of life. Find out how:

◆ After she lost her job, Nona S., fifty, a former news producer and charity celebrity recruiter, overcame the stigma of "being overqualified" and volunteered her way into multiple full-time offers.

◆ An interim executive placement worked for Stephen F., fifty-nine, who wanted to return to his longtime career in academia and enjoy professional payoff without the office headaches.

◆ A broken ankle and free small-business classes inspired Marianne D. to give up her twenty-five-year accounting career and follow her dream of opening a quilt shop.

◆ In middle age, a former Seaworld marketing exec and father of six uncovered a hidden artistic talent and turned the nightmare of an unexpected layoff into a $4-million-a-year business.

◆ Gerry B., fifty-three, negotiated early retirement and walked away from a fifteen-year stint as an HR executive to forge a career that would bring him closer to home and improve his quality of life.

◆ Stay-at-home mom Sharai R. employed a step-by-step approach—from college classes to volunteering to part-time work—to successfully re-enter the workforce after a twenty-year absence.

How to
Find a Job After 50

How to Find a Job After 50

From Part-Time to Full-Time, from Career Moves to New Careers

BETSY CUMMINGS

WARNER
BUSINESS
BOOKS ™

NEW YORK • BOSTON

This publication is designed to provide competent and reliable information regarding the subject matter covered. However, it is sold with the understanding that the author and publisher are not engaged in rendering legal, financial, or other professional advice. Laws and practices often vary from state to state and if legal or other expert assistance is required, the services of a professional should be sought. The author and publisher specifically disclaim any liability that is incurred from the use or application of the contents of this book.

Warner Business Books
Warner Books

Time Warner Book Group
1271 Avenue of the Americas, New York, NY 10020
Visit our Web site at www.twbookmark.com.

The Warner Business Books logo is a trademark of Warner Books.

Printed in the United States of America

First Edition: October 2005
10 9 8 7 6 5 4 3 2 1

Library of Congress Cataloging-in-Publication Data
Cummings, Betsy.
    How to find a job after 50 : from part-time to full-time, from career moves to new careers / Betsy Cummings.—1st ed.
        p. cm.
    ISBN 0-446-69539-4
1. Job hunting—United States.   2. Baby boom generation—Employment—United States.   3. Middle aged persons—Employment—United States. 4. Older people—Employment—United States.   5. Career changes—United States.   6. Self-evaluation—United States.   I. Title.
    HF5382.75.U6C85 2005
    650.14'084'60973   2005010558

Acknowledgments

Just like finding a dream job, writing a book takes any number of interviews, as well as an enormous amount of effort and assistance, from folks without whose help this book would not have been possible.

I'd like to thank my editor Rick Wolff at Warner Books, who so generously gave me the opportunity to write about such a compelling topic, one that is rapidly becoming a point of focus for one of America's largest populations. He helped define more clearly the content of this book, and with his guidance the final product has evolved into a rich resource for mature job seekers.

Thanks to Melinda Ligos for her tireless support and encouragement during the relentless race that was this book. As much as an editor, every writer needs a mentor, a role Melinda has served for me for many years.

Jeri Sedlar provided invaluable insights into the baby boomer generation as well as an impressive understanding of what's at stake in the job market for Americans over fifty. A huge thank-you to Nancy Thompson and Deborah Russell at AARP, and Colin Milner at the International Council on Active Aging, who provided countless studies, data, and reports that helped build a statistical foundation for a good deal of the book's research.

Eric Kingson, a professor of social work and public administration at Syracuse University, has been helpful on a number of work-related pieces I've researched in addition to this book. He always provides sound insight and discussion on the topic of older workers.

The online job site Monster.com provided much-needed job-hunting and résumé-rewriting tips for which I am grateful. A special thanks to Monster founder and chairman Jeff Taylor for his—as usual—candid remarks about the state of America's job market and outlook on the future of work in this country. Such forthcoming, honest dialogue can be a rare find for reporters. Jeff is always a rich resource in that regard.

A tremendous thank-you to John Berry, who listened more than anyone while this book was being written. He provided more support than I ever imagined one person could offer.

Finally, I'd like to thank the countless individuals fifty and over who so readily shared their stories of struggle and success in rich detail so that readers could be moved to find the job that most inspires them. Their stories prove that there's a dream job for every older worker—and that it's entirely possible to find it.

Contents

Introduction

The Fifty-Year-Old Wake-Up Call

In the past year, more than five hundred thousand Americans began their workday gainfully employed and walked out at the end of the day without a job. Fired, laid off, forced out as the victim of a company closure, or otherwise shown the door, millions of workers, plenty of them over the age of fifty, were suddenly forced to reenter the job search market, something many hadn't faced for years, some not for decades.

Others simply walked out on their own, uninspired by what they do, desperate to escape the restrictions of tight management, or anxious to find a new career path—or at least a job that will offer them a different professional role or challenge.

Regardless of how they got there, embarking on a job hunt can be daunting and, for those ill prepared, a quick lesson in humility, frustration, or despair. Never an easy proposition, finding a job after the age of fifty can be disheartening for some and overwhelming, even terrifying for others. Résumés not looked at in years may need to be completely reworked. Interviewing skills have likely all but dried up. Networking—probably the most feared professional task next to public speaking—is something few job seekers are willing to embrace.

What's more, if you haven't traveled the job-hunting circuit in recent years, you may not be aware of the many resources that have sprung up out there in the last year or two alone. Classified advertising certainly still exists. And it shouldn't be knocked— people land jobs every day by scanning the listings in their local newspaper. But where job seekers might once have been able to rely on that historically reliable source alone, now it's just the tip of the job-hunting iceberg—and barely that. Classifieds can be the *last* spot a company places a listing for a position, especially if the job is in a niche industry where online job boards focused on a particular skill or area of expertise may more effectively target the talent that a company is seeking.

The good news, however, is that older workers do have a vast, rich pool of resources they may not have been aware of, may have taken for granted, or may simply have overlooked. And that pertains to far more than just job postings. Longtime employment in a particular industry provides reams of contacts for job seekers, but many applicants don't immediately consider that option when they start looking for work. Industry groups can help out-of-work job hunters realize what areas of an industry might be easiest to tap for job openings. Association memberships throughout the years can now pay off in contacts and job leads.

The best tactic for mature job seekers? Stop before you panic, and consider all the contacts, resources, and avenues of exploration your career has built to date. Those who do are usually pleasantly surprised with not only the options they have but also the opportunities they never imagined lay ahead.

To be certain, the workplace after fifty is a rich terrain. For all its uncertainty—careers winding down, retirement looming, a younger generation itching to fill spots soon to be vacated by older workers—the opportunity for professional growth has never been more robust for Americans over fifty than it is today. And for good reason. "People now are living on average thirty years longer," says Jeri Sedlar, a retirement expert and co-author of *Don't Retire, Rewire!*, a book about finding fulfilling work later in life. And they're looking to fill those years with meaningful work or make sure that they have work options so their finances don't dry up.

If thirty or more years of living beyond age fifty is the case for most Americans, older workers suddenly faced with a pink slip would be wise to consider the many decades of living that probably lie ahead of them. But they should also realize that there are numerous opportunities for older job seekers in need of employment later in life. Don't lose hope; older workers are a much more desired talent pool than you may think.

That's good news for workers over fifty who are suddenly unemployed but aren't thinking about how they can make early retirement work. Most Americans in that age range don't have the luxury of hanging up their career after being told to clean out their desk and say good-bye. Expenses usually demand that people put in years more of work. In addition, more Americans are also realizing how crucial their jobs are to their physical and mental well-being.

In interviews conducted for this book with dozens of senior workers—from as young as 50 to as old as 104—all, without fail, stressed that they couldn't feel fulfilled financially, professionally, intellectually, socially, or emotionally without some form of work in their later years.

Where to Go from Here?

That's the question of the hour on the lips of many older workers who have walked off the job or been asked to leave their place of employment in recent years.

For better or worse, you've found yourself at a crossroads. Whether it's a devastating layoff or an intentional walkout from a painful position, you now have the opportunity to rework your career from this point forward.

To change careers, find a new job, or return to work after years away, especially at this stage in life, it pays to discover what really turns you on, what drives you day in and day out, what's going to propel you into another profession, and what could motivate a monumental change in your professional life.

That requires some serious personal exploration. Workers in this age group are asking themselves the following:

- How do I really want to spend the next twenty to thirty years of my life, now that I can realistically expect to do so?
- Where can I continue to showcase my talents and be appreciated and compensated for doing so?
- How can I step away from an all-consuming, high-pressure career, but still keep a hand in the profession that I find compelling?
- What's more important to me now—lifestyle or professional growth?
- How much do I need to work to maintain my current quality of life?
- What effect will my professional change have on my family?

These are important questions.

Baby boomers' lives aren't without their hurdles. As they enter their fifties, they could just as easily start forging a path to retirement as they could one toward new professional ambitions. But doing the latter might seem like an easier path for those who are young, eager, and untainted by the economic, political, financial, and social frustrations of corporate life. Changing paths now requires tapping energy—whether it's sparked by a newfound interest, panic over lost employment, or the possibility of a new lease on your professional life.

That energy will be widely needed as older workers face other possible hurdles in pursuing new avenues. Plenty of potential employers, for example, are wary of older workers, whom they fear might be more feeble, less mentally alert, less ambitious, or more apt to suffer from health problems than younger colleagues. Experts on aging insist that those perceptions are untrue. The good news is that the eagerness with which companies are retaining a mature workforce is a refreshing sign that employees in their fifties and beyond are an increasingly valued and important part of American business success.

Even for those managers who still don't have faith in the strength of older workers, human resource executives are slowly working to change the perceptions rooted deep within company offices. Consider a recent study from the Society for Human Resource Management (SHRM), which showed that:

- 72 percent of human resource professionals said older workers provide invaluable experience.
- 69 percent said they had a stronger work ethic than younger workers.
- 68 percent said they were more reliable employees.

If ageism still exists in American offices today, it may not be able to for long—and rightly so. **Over the next two decades, seventy-six million baby boomers will approach retirement—** leaving behind a mammoth gap and talent drain in corporate America. Predictions are that over the next ten years, the fastest-growing workforce age group will be made up of those fifty-five and older. At the same time, according to the Bureau of Labor Statistics, the number of jobs available in the market will increase by 15 percent, or twenty-two million jobs, by 2010, but the labor force will only offer an additional seventeen million candidates. This means that if boomers aren't a highly desirable talent pool now, they will be in the near future—in fact, they will comprise a necessary recruitment population for companies looking to fill gaps in the workforce with already trained and skilled workers.

Some in corporate America are taking steps now to help older workers break new ground as they navigate an evolving workplace. Companies such as Procter & Gamble have realized the value of former employees and are bringing them back to tap their skills and expertise on a part-time basis. Companies such as the Aerospace Corporation, a research and development company

WORKFORCE GROWTH PER AGE GROUP BY 2010

Workers 25 and younger	2 percent
Workers 25–34	−5 percent
Workers 35–44	−19 percent
Workers 45–54	8 percent
Workers 55-plus	33 percent

Source: Department of Health and Human Services.

in El Segundo, California, have established phased-retirement programs that allow older workers to gradually step away from their careers over months or years. Others, such as Ford Motor Company, offer part-time programs in which employees can reduce the number of hours they work each week.

Recent surveys indicate that older workers are interested in at least some form of adjustment to their work schedule. For many, that may mean working part time or flex time. A Watson Wyatt survey released in 2004 polled one thousand workers between ages fifty and seventy; two-thirds noted that they wanted to phase out of their current employer. And if companies want to keep workers longer, recruit them back, or make certain they don't jump ship for the competition, which may offer a more enticing work environment, they should begin now to craft strategies that cater to older workers. Certain industries, such as education, health care, and manufacturing, are more receptive to phasing and other flexible work options.

Leveraging Years of Experience

Despite a rash of lost jobs and a seemingly bleak job market in recent years, experts have repeatedly insisted that older workers are gaining power and influence in the workplace—and are securing more promising work opportunities as a result.

But there's an individual push going on as well. Much of the effort to continue working is coming from older workers punished by a market that tanked after the dot-com boom. Others trying to make do in retirement without an income are finding themselves blowing through the nest egg at an alarming rate. And perhaps more than anything, older workers are realizing that if they are living longer, they'll want to be more engaged in their later years and look for ways to find life inspiring. The typical post-career life activities, such as bridge, golf, and gardening, may not cut it.

"It's a necessity to work and create mental stimulation in older people," says Colin Milner, CEO of the International Council on Active Aging. "Work is a great thing dollar-wise, but it offers a variety of different elements that you need to live. It stimulates your mind, keeps you socially connected. It's much more than a purpose."

Indeed, more and more Americans are discovering that work is a key part of moving into the next stage of their lives.

Making a Move

If you think the end of the road is near in your current job or line of work, but aren't sure, ask yourself the following:

- If I'm not happy in my current job, what is it that I'd rather be doing?
- Is there something I could change about my current work situation that would make it better—maybe working fewer hours or participating in more inspiring projects?
- Am I ready to leave the camaraderie of peers and work on my own or do I simply want a new environment with similar work elements and structure?
- Are there any more challenging positions or levels of responsibility that I could tap at this company or in my line of work elsewhere?

- Have I learned all that I can in this profession, or are there areas still unexplored that could provide new career growth?
- Would I be bored not coming to work every day?
- Could I change my job or work hours and still maintain my current lifestyle and cost of living?
- Is there much salary growth left for me at my company?
- Is there a company in my field that would provide better growth and money opportunities than my current employer?
- Would it pay to try my same position in another industry?

If none of these answers comes easily, then chances are you need to search deeper within yourself to find what drives you professionally day in and day out. If professional ambition has never been your strong suit, be honest about it. Maybe rethinking your career or work life isn't about finding a new job or career—maybe it's about holding on to the one you already have. Perhaps finding a similar job in your line of work and simply building a retirement portfolio or boosting the one you've already got is more important than discovering a new professional commitment at this stage of your life. Forcing yourself to revamp a professional career later in life will only be an exercise in frustration and disappointment if you're not professionally driven in the first place.

One other thing to keep in mind: Be flexible while investigating new career and work options. **Where once almost all Americans imagined themselves not working in their sixties or seventies, a large group of us now see new work opportunities.** Likewise, your vision for working later in life or during retirement may change many times before you settle on what it is you really want to do.

"My vision has changed tremendously," says Robert Cannon, fifty-six, who opened his Cannon Advantage business consultancy later in life and watched an array of people throughout his career travel down various paths toward retirement. "It was sad to see so many people hanging on and counting the days until they could retire and get out of wherever it was they were," he continues. "I've seen others quit cold turkey and they don't have anything else to do. And yet I've seen others who have stayed involved. One man is eighty-five and still actively working. He called me to talk about my helping him on another project. This man plays tennis every week, mows his own lawn, and still is looking forward to life where so many others are ready to roll up and die."

PART I

Baby Boomers and the Changing Workplace

Chapter 1

The Value of Older Workers

As millions of mature workers exit the labor market in the next two decades, the good news, of course, is that older workers will be in greater demand—and will be the point of focus of corporate recruitment and retention programs. **"I'm expecting the worst labor shortage of our lifetime," says Jeff Taylor, founder and chairman of online job site Monster.com.** "If you look at the actual numbers, you have about seventy million baby boomers who are going to retire between now and 2015 and only thirty million younger workers to take their place at the entry level."

At places like Deere & Company, for example, 50 percent of employees are expected to retire within a decade, according to the American Association of Retired Persons (AARP). The company is currently taking a very proactive approach to becoming more appealing to older employees through recruitment and retention programs targeted specifically at mature workers.

It's hard to imagine such a drastic shortage now in a market that has seen companies shed millions of people in corporate downsizings while job creation has been lethargic at best. But a mass exodus of the boomers currently in the workforce could have such an effect. Experiencing a skill shortage, as companies did during the late-1990s dot-com boom, was stressful for employers but not impossible to manage. A body shortage is another matter entirely.

According to Taylor, "Corporations know how to recruit around skills, such as nursing, but when they start having body shortages, corporations are not prepared to manage through that." The answer could largely lie with retaining or recruiting employees in their career twilight years. Firms that don't might see disastrous results. "We're going to see a trend where companies go out of business because they don't know how to recruit and retain employees," Taylor predicts. Even with jobs moving offshore and overseas, companies will have a hard time filling positions. "The actual number of jobs offshore in places like India is only 1 to 2 percent" of U.S. employees, for instance—and with millions of positions potentially being vacated by retiring boomers, it's clear that outsourcing won't even begin to fill the gap. "We had 1.4 million information technology openings in 1999, and corporations were in a dead panic," Taylor says. Boost that number to ten million in the coming decade and some companies may be sent into a staffing tailspin.

The good news for older workers, then, is that they'll have more leverage to craft the career they envision later in life—whether that vision consists of full-time work, part-time employment on their terms, jobs with flexible hours, or other individually crafted work opportunities. We may not see the free cars and fifty-thousand-dollar signing bonuses of the dot-com era; nor does the looming labor shortage mean workers fifty and over can saunter into an employer's office any day soon, spew a litany of demands, and expect all of them to be met. But it does mean they don't have to feel as though they've been cast off for a younger generation.

Young workers will always be a highly sought-after employee population, but after working with older employees with more frequency through retiree recruitment programs, many companies are realizing how valuable a labor resource they are and are eager to hire more. **Certain industries—including telecommunications and security services—are already seeking out older workers for their reliability and work ethic.**

Cathy Fyock, an employment strategist in Crestwood, Kentucky, and an expert on older workers, notes the success of an initiative she helped create as a human resource executive for a national fast-food restaurant chain several years ago. Restaurant managers were complaining that they couldn't hold on to employees for long; their businesses were suffering under enormous staff turnover. But when HR professionals sent older applicants to apply for jobs at the restaurants, managers turned them away—"because they were old," Fyock says.

So company headquarters started pressuring managers to hire workers in that age group. The reaction, when managers finally did, was astounding. "They would call us and say, 'This person is working out so well, we have to get another one,'" Fyock notes. "Until that positive experience, managers were dead set against older workers. It's amazing that we can be so biased against something that with any luck we're all going to reach ourselves someday."

Managers in various other fields are coming to appreciate older workers, too. Temporary agency Veritude in Boston has noted an increasing number of corporate clients requesting older workers for jobs such as call center support. "Older workers are a very rich source of talent for our customers," says Linda Stewart, executive vice president at Veritude.

Joanne Fritz, an expert on mature workers and founder of the Web site NotYetRetired.com, recalls a security company specifically requesting older workers when screening job applicants for security shifts at office buildings. No experience was needed—the company simply wanted a population that would consistently show up for work and be diligent about their duties. Security managers said they had noticed such desirable work traits—low turnover, responsible behavior, conscientious attitudes, and infrequent sick days—more consistently in older workers than among the younger security officers they hired.

And there are other indicators that opportunities for older workers are expanding. Just look at the explosion of Web sites over the past several years developed to help older job seekers tap a market that increasingly needs their talent and expertise. ThePhoenixLink.com, for example, connects older workers with recruiters for mid- to senior-level management positions. Bill Vick, the site's founder and owner, named his firm for the rising Phoenix of mythology, to represent the rising stock of older employees in the American workplace. Perhaps he's on to something: The site has three thousand registered users and averages fifteen million viewed pages a month. Such sites are important for older workers suffering under the mass layoffs occurring over the past few years. Other online job boards geared toward workers over fifty offer that audience a place to feel their specific employment issues are being addressed.

But do these job boards for seniors work better than general job-hunting sites, such as Monster, CareerBuilder, or HotJobs, which cast a wide net and list a varied array of postings for job seekers of all ages? Not necessarily. While the Senior Job Bank and its counterparts may offer more jobs targeted specifically to seniors, general sites also feature sections devoted entirely to older workers, covering topics from landing part-time jobs to fighting ageism and working abroad. Monster, for example, has an entire section dedicated to diversity and older workers. Plus a majority of recruiters spend more time perusing the better-known boards. And actual samples on Monster and similar sites of how résumés, for example, can be reworked are extremely useful in putting together materials for an effective job search.

Tapping Older Workers

When any new trend or movement hits a culture, resources pop up to meet its needs. That's just as true with the older-worker job search. Google the terms "jobs" and "older worker" and hundreds of thousands of responses pop up.

The information on these sites can be invaluable. Eric Summers, founder and director of the Senior Job Bank, tells the story of a retired printer who was so despondent over his lack of job options that he became suicidal. "He posted a résumé on seniorjobbank.com and within a day got the right job around the corner from him," Summers says. "His children sent me five hundred dollars because I saved their father's life."

That may be an uncommon tale, but experts say senior job boards can do much to help older workers—if only by making them aware that there are plenty of groups interested in their talents and work experience. And older applicants can do much to enhance their job search by using them effectively. The keys are to search many of them and often; use their available articles, research, and links to your advantage; and figure out ways the sites can get you connected to other job seekers, industry contacts, and people who can help get you farther down your career path. Don't just wait for postings, send in your résumé, and sit back hoping for a call. Be proactive on job boards. Join discussion groups, post your résumé, network with peers online. Job searches are a numbers game: **The more people and leads you can connect with, the more likely you are to get an offer.**

Job Sites for Older Workers

Where can you find online job resources if you're fifty-plus? The following list—while nowhere near exhaustive—will get you started on some of the most popular older-worker job boards and summarize the services they offer. As you move around these sites, you'll realize which are best suited to your needs.

◆ **Retired Brains**, www.retiredbrains.com. This site connects senior workers with employers looking to hire people for full-time, part-time, or temporary positions that require little to no training. A job search for accountants, for example, showed everything from fifteen-dollar-an-hour jobs to six-figure full-time positions. You'll also find résumé-writing services, information on continuing education programs nationwide, free trade publications, and links and phone numbers for fifty volunteer organizations. The site's Senior Resource Center offers links to government, retirement planning, insurance, and other sites helpful to older Americans.

◆ **The Phoenix Link**, www.thephoenixlink.com, offers interim and full-time management positions for technology workers and executives. There are live chat rooms and online forums for users to discuss career and job issues. Career books are available through an online bookstore, and you can participate in virtual training workshops or create an electronic résumé with streaming video.

♦ **The Senior Job Bank**, www.seniorjobbank.org. Focused almost entirely on job listings rather than job-seeker services, the Senior Job Bank provides detailed listings of jobs by state. Positions tend to be entry level to midmanagement.

♦ **Maturity Works**, www.maturityworks.org. Sponsored by the National Council on the Aging, this site is a rich resource for aging information, although very few jobs are listed.

♦ **Executive Interim Management**, www.interimmgt.us, is a staffing firm that places high-level executives in interim positions for companies that need top-tier execs to help them through transitions.

♦ **Experience Works**, www.experienceworks.org. Focused on helping lower-income older workers find employment, Experience Works places many people who have never worked into jobs via training programs or nonprofit organizations.

♦ **Boomer Career**, www.boomercareer.com. This robust site and online newsletter offers everything from tips on résumé writing to job postings to discussions on the fear of changing jobs. You'll find content on the work–life balance, financial planning, and starting a business. A free membership is required to access the site's content.

♦ **Senior Service America**, www.seniorserviceamerica.org, trains and places older workers in community service jobs. It also includes an online news section with the latest information on age-related issues.

♦ **Monster**, www.monster.com. A special section on older workers within Monster's diversity section is specifically geared toward older workers and offers a wealth of practical, detailed tips on searching for jobs, acing interviews, battling ageism, and other vital tools for finding a job after fifty.

◆ **Quintessential Careers**, www.quintcareers.com. Geared for all ages, this Web site offers online searches for jobs. An equally strong feature is articles that provide advice for older workers on everything from networking to job hunting.

◆ **Senior Help Wanted**, www.seniorhelpwanted.com, is a comprehensive job board with a smattering of postings for positions from day laborers to executives.

◆ **The Retired Worker**, www.theretiredworker.com. This site's job postings are specifically for part-time, temporary, or contract workers. It also offers online discussion forums about various work topics as well as an e-newsletter.

◆ **First Gov for Seniors**, www.firstgov.gov. A government-sponsored Web site that offers postings for federal jobs along with volunteer opportunities.

◆ **Seniors for Hire**, www.seniors4hire.org, claims to be the number one site online for U.S. job seekers over fifty, and offers information on resources and articles along with job listings. It also includes links to other senior, non-job-related Web sites.

◆ **Jobs for Seniors Meet Up**, www.jobsforseniors.meetup.com. Here you'll find a listing of cities worldwide (but mostly within the United States) where meetings are held in which seniors can network with other older job seekers.

◆ **Retire Careers**, www.retirecareers.com, has job postings, online résumé-building tips, and capabilities to search for information about various companies.

In addition to these sites, don't forget to check the job boards directly on a company's Web site. These listings are sometimes more up to date, and applying directly to a company can help you avoid being inundated by headhunters who cruise through online job boards looking to fill their recruitment quotas with job seekers. You're also one step closer to the actual person who will do the hiring. And it keeps your name in front of the company's HR personnel, who more than likely will keep your résumé on file and periodically review it for other positions that become available.

Debunking Older-Worker Myths

Not every employer understands the need for older talent in the coming years, nor are they all open to the idea of hiring older workers over younger ones. "There's certainly discrimination" against older workers, according to Colin Milner of the International Council on Active Aging.

Sadly, Milner's right—age discrimination is alive and well in corporate America. "Employers are not interested in hiring seniors because they don't want to pay expensive health benefits that seniors create," says Art Koff, founder of RetiredBrains.com, a job and resource Web site for older workers. Or at least that's the impression that many companies have about senior workers.

But there may be a more fundamental reason, notes aging expert Cathy Fyock. "People don't want to face their own mortality. Seeing someone older somehow, even on a subconscious level, makes an individual realize that they will be there someday, too, and they don't want to face that."

That may or may not be, but whatever fuels ageism in the workplace is at play now, according to many older job seekers.

Nona Snyder, fifty, knows the feeling all too well. For two decades she had a thriving career, spending fourteen years as a producer for programs such as ABC's *World News Tonight,* then later working as the head of celebrity recruitment for the March of Dimes, and finally as head of the American Cancer Society.

Surely her résumé is one that opens doors for her. But since losing her job following a restructuring at the ACS, Snyder has found little to no employment. In interview after interview with more than forty companies in the past three years, she's heard phrases like "You're overqualified"; "Won't you be bored?"; and "We'll be in touch" time and again from employers that she is convinced are not interested in hiring someone her age, particularly when she is competing against applicants fifteen years or more her junior.

Those kinds of lines are a refrain heard all too commonly from employers today in businesses across the country, Fyock agrees, because they offer employers a way to explain away why an older worker may not be suitable for a position without being accused of discriminatory practices. But the politically correct phrases are so fraught with unstated messages that even the Equal Employment Opportunity Commission (EEOC) has taken notice, ruling that such statements—especially ones about being overqualified—can possibly be considered cases for age discrimination.

On Snyder's part, the job hunt has gotten so desperate that she's found herself in temporary agencies being interviewed by twenty-year-olds for receptionist jobs that pay eighteen thousand dollars a year. "I never hear back from them," Snyder says. A colleague of hers experienced a similar job hunt after a career as a television producer and is now a secretary in a Washington, DC, dentist's office.

Luckily for Snyder, her efforts are starting to pay off. Volunteering at a local hospital and museum eventually landed her multiple interviews for full-time directorial positions—something she says came about quickly after she demonstrated her skills through volunteer work. She's hopeful that, several interviews later, she'll receive an offer shortly.

Will the position offer the salary she once enjoyed? Probably not, Snyder predicts. But there are plenty of other perks that she says she'll be delighted with. "It's a new world we live in and it's about benefits, benefits, benefits. I'm compromising and I've learned that doing so is part of the whole package. Plus, the hours are good, so the job will leave me free time to do what I want to do on my own."

Can the perception that Snyder faced about older workers being antiquated really be that pervasive? Is this movement by older workers to reengage themselves in new or former careers doing nothing to banish such myths? The short answer is that discrimination still exists. The good news is that it's being diminished more and more.

Slowly, organizations such as AARP are correcting misperceptions—that older workers are less sharp, less reliable, more likely to have health problems—that have persisted for years, even though many companies are reluctant to let those stereotypes go. Older workers, for their part, might argue that younger generations have a weaker work ethic, feel an unwarranted sense of entitlement, and expect significant compensation for little to no work, while having little loyalty to their employers. More important, Milner says, the undesirable outcomes that can result from the draining of corporate America's talent pool are beginning to dawn on executives: "Companies are beginning to realize the aging of America is happening, and because of that fewer workers are going to be around."

Until the day when full realization hits, however, there are definitely some tricks to combating age discrimination during interviews:

◆ **Play Up Your Experience.** You've got years of working under your belt—now's the time to exploit them. If nothing else, experience is the one advantage you have over younger job seekers going after the same position. Highlight any unique talents you've developed over time that you think a younger person may not have.

◆ **Appear Younger.** No, not by dressing in leather low riders with your newly pierced belly button on full display. Show that you are keeping up with the times. Seek out the innovators—or at least the latest innovations—in your chosen field. Keep up on current news in the industry or profession in which you're looking to work. Attend industry conferences, association meetings, and other events in your area that may offer insight into your chosen field.

◆ **Emphasize Your Professionalism.** Ageism isn't a one-way street. There are typecasts that exist among younger workers as well, and for every stereotype an employer may project onto older workers, there exists an equal stereotype of younger job seekers. Now may be the time to emphasize your reliability, proven performance level, and overall track record over a long-term career.

◆ **Be Flexible.** Part of the problem with the interviewing process for older workers, particularly those who have held upper-level management positions, is that employers assume they won't settle for anything but a job at the same level. Moreover, some interviewers may assume that older job seekers come to the office with a set management style and rigid view of how things should be run. So it's important during the interview to talk about and emphasize your willingness to start out on a lower level, work under the supervision of someone ten years your junior, or operate within a flexible management style.

♦ **Play It Cool.** That doesn't mean aloof or ridiculously younger than you actually are. But it doesn't hurt to put on a calm, reasoned, casual demeanor during the interview. Don't overdo it and seem lackadaisical, but it's important for a potential employer to realize that just because you're a little older doesn't mean you're incapable of rolling with the punches, or have become too structured and formatted in your approach to work.

Breaking the Bias Barriers

Unfortunately, age discrimination is an inevitable part of the job hunt for older workers. **The key to overcoming ageist biases is to predict and counteract them,** given the fact that any politically correct HR professional won't mention them outright. If you can recognize some of the more common biases, you'll be better prepared to fight them off. They include, but aren't limited to:

♦ You are older, so you're less healthy—that may mean more sick days and less productivity.

♦ You can't take criticism or supervision from someone younger than you.

◆ You have developed a rigid management or work style after so many years in the workplace, and you're either not open to trying new methods or slow in learning them.

◆ The chances of you sticking around for very long are slim to none, since you've probably got one foot in the retirement door already.

◆ You're obviously out of touch with the latest technology.

◆ Your age is going to seriously up the cost of benefits.

◆ You lack energy and physical stamina.

◆ You're not willing to start at the bottom and work your way up.

◆ A generation gap will prevent you from forming productive interpersonal relationships in the office with younger co-workers.

◆ Clients will associate the company with an older face—and possibly a more dated image in the market.

◆ Your ideas are from an earlier time and out of touch with today's industry.

The Advantage of Age

For all the barriers that older workers face and fight off as they interview for jobs where employers may exhibit unfair biases against them, **there are plenty of benefits to being an older worker that people over fifty can use in their favor.** Workers who have specific or high-level skills sharpened over a twenty-

or thirty-year career, for example, can have invaluable expertise. And those who fit that bill are highly sought to resolve pressing business issues.

At Executive Interim Management, former executives from companies such as General Electric, who are now semiretired, are placed in high-level assignments on an interim basis, often nine months to a year. "We're not doing an executive search, because our clients need a response time in a week or two," says Roger Sweeney, executive director of the organization, which has been operating in the United States for five years but has roots in Europe that go back two decades. Instead, Sweeney is pulling from a roster of highly skilled executives who can be inserted into a company at a moment's notice to help deal with major management issues.

"We're overkilling" the clients with talent, Sweeney says. "We're bringing in a heavyweight person who is stepping down in assignment and doesn't expect to make the same money as when they were employed full time, but still wants to be compensated well for the job they are doing." Typical situations include mergers and acquisitions, corporate downsizings, and other management crises that call for objective, hard-and-fast professional decisions. The New York office fills about ten interim positions a year, compared with forty or fifty in major European cities. "This is still a new idea to the U.S.," Sweeney admits. But it is certainly catching on.

"Interim executive assignments are gaining in value these days for a number of reasons," says Joseph Daniel McCool, editor in chief of *Executive Recruiter News* (a product of Kennedy Information publishing and research company). "An interim exec comes with less risk than a permanent hire, they're easier to disentangle from an organization if they don't fit into the culture of the employer, and there are more experienced executives looking for these short-term opportunities." In short, there's better talent available on the fly today.

A March 2004 survey by Kennedy Information of the fifty largest executive-recruiting firms suggests older executives may be searching more often for this type of work today. The study found that 26 percent of executive recruiters seek out part-time jobs for executives, largely for those getting out of their careers. That's an increase of 7 percent in just one year, McCool says.

And it's not just former business executives. Nonprofit and academic arenas are using interim staff as well. The Registry for College and University Presidents places former heads of schools in interim positions that last two or three years. Stephen Fritz, fifty-nine, has been with the registry since 2000 after spending fourteen years on an executive level within private institutions, most recently at Hiwassee College in Madisonville, Tennessee. A brief foray into stockbrokerage didn't provide him the satisfaction that he had felt in academia: It promised to be a "nice opportunity," Fritz says, and "a good break from the academic world. But after a few years, I missed the academic world and missed working with younger folks."

Going back to college seemed important, but Fritz wasn't certain about going back full time. That's when he discovered the registry and the flexibility of finding work on an interim basis. Now he's the interim dean of arts and sciences at Point Park College in Pittsburgh, helping to bring the school up to "university status" and develop a college of arts and sciences. Before that he was an interim president at Goddard College in Plainfield, Vermont, strengthening a failing school that was financially devastated.

The interim work allows Fritz enough involvement to become invested in the schools he works at but not overwhelmed by the atmosphere there. "I'm allowed to be totally objective," he says. "It's the opportunity to make a significant contribution without having to worry about the politics, about what my job's going to look like, and how I can position myself for the next five to ten years."

In other words, it gives him immense professional enjoyment without the office headaches. It's a work strategy he sees himself using for at least the next five to ten years. Under this work plan, Fritz says, "I don't have to worry about competing for tenure or locking in a long stay at a school that will lead to a nice, comfortable retirement."

Signs Older Workers Are Welcome

On the surface, it's not always easy to tell if a potential employer is eager to hire older workers. Age discrimination is, of course, illegal, but it doesn't stop a lot of companies from making biased judgments against older job seekers, masked by statements that the older workers "weren't as qualified." Other than locating lists of companies known to be friendly to mature workers (plenty can be found on the AARP Web site), there are a few positive signs that AARP says older workers can look for as they search for employment. These are not guarantees that companies are actually actively recruiting or hiring job seekers over fifty, but they can usually be taken as encouraging signs by applicants within that age group that a company is friendly to older workers:

- Job listings specifically mention the need for maturity and work experience.
- Ads for positions are listed on Web sites known to be frequented by older workers or people of varying ages.
- Various types of training are available to workers of any age, and older workers are encouraged to participate.
- The company's benefits program includes extensive prescription drug coverage as well as extra long-term care insurance and short- and long-term disability insurance.
- Pension plans are clearly defined for long-term employees.
- Flexible work options, such as flex time, telecommuting, and time off for family needs, are available for all employee age groups.
- Phased-retirement programs have been implemented.
- Former employees are encouraged to return to work on a part-time basis.

Source: AARP Best Employers for Workers Over 50.

And, indeed, some companies are:

- Adecco Employment Services, a career counseling and placement agency in Melville, New York, offers temporary jobs to its employees as a bridge to retirement.
- DaVita, Inc., a health care company in Torrance, California, offers flex-time schedules and tuition reimbursement to employees.
- The Hartford Financial Services Group, Inc., in Hartford, Connecticut, has created eight flexible work programs for staff, including phased retirement.

- New York Life Insurance Company, in New York, has a child care center for grandchildren.
- Mitretek Systems, Inc., an engineering firm in Falls Church, Virginia, provides career counseling for employees of all ages.

Service from Every Level

If there's an equalizer in business, it's the uncertainty of life after a layoff. From high-powered executive to midlevel manager to factory floor worker, what job opportunities lie ahead are anyone's guess. It might seem that executives would be better connected with the inside track to potential jobs through corporate and industry networking. But a seemingly endless trail of stories tells a different tale. One marketing executive let go after his company went bust in the dot-com boom spent nine months looking for a job. Of course, the state of an economy has as much to do with a person's job-hunting success as anything— something clearly not working for *any* employee on *any* level after a bubble bursts.

Blue-collar workers, whose skills can be highly specialized and suitable only for niche markets, may find job opportunities less bountiful after mass layoffs, versus marketing managers who can transfer many of their skills from one job to the next or even one industry to another. Blue-collar workers also may face on-the-job injury and other hurdles their white-collar colleagues don't, which can permanently prevent them from finding gainful employment.

Inevitably, another problem seems to occur in the face of serious job loss among blue-collar workers: Their plight is overlooked. Sweeping layoffs of white-collar, midtier managers at major corporations are front-page news, while factory layoffs in the hundreds or thousands, though worthy of coverage by national press, are often analyzed more out of concern for a company's market viability than for the number of people whose regular paychecks have suddenly been eliminated.

But even abysmal economies may not be all bad for blue-collar workers, including those in their fifties. Temporary work, for example, has seen vast growth in the past few years (up 18.6 percent since November 2001, according to the Economic Policy Institute), suggesting there may be steady jobs for blue-collar workers who can pick up temporary assignments.

"It's unlikely you'll hire a senior for a forklift driver, but you could hire a mechanic on a project basis—hourly or salaried—who has some managerial experience," says Art Koff.

Service Jobs Promising Strong Growth in the Next Ten Years

In addition to identifying companies that are open to hiring people over fifty, finding work might be easier if you pursue professions or positions in which older workers have a better chance of becoming employed. What follows is by no means a complete list of such jobs, but it is a snapshot of where older workers are more likely to find jobs in the workplace:

- ◆ Customer service representative.

- ◆ Teaching assistant.

- ◆ Teacher.

- ◆ Retail salesperson.

- Landscaper/groundskeeper.

- Cashier.

- Computer support specialist.

- Real estate agent.

- Secretary/receptionist.

- Truck driver/courier.

- Bookkeeper/accounting clerk.

- Child care worker.

Source: AARP.

Chapter 2

Leaving the Workplace

As more and more older workers approach retirement—currently **14 percent of the workforce is fifty-five and older, and this number is expected to rise to 19 percent by 2012,** according to AARP—when and how to leave your current job can be as tough a decision as deciding what to do after exiting. "This is a time in life that has reached a new focus partly because we age more slowly now and we age more healthfully," says Christine Millen, a former executive at Deloitte Consulting, then Deloitte & Touche, who tussled with her own post-career plans before founding the Transition Network for women over fifty. "We now have a serious thirty years between fifty and becoming frail and elderly."

Typically, the notion has been that older workers start to feel less professional and financial stress later in their careers. The mortgage is paid, the kids are out of school, and the financial pressures that existed earlier aren't as pressing.

But these days, numerous older employees are making a new realization in an increasingly volatile economy: that retirement can, ironically, bring its own element of stress to a person's life—figuring out what to do with so much free time, readjusting to having no daily schedule, and otherwise feeling that your sense of purpose—your job—has just been eliminated.

Recently, new stresses, such as deflated portfolios, decreasing faith in traditional investments, and international political and economic volatility, are combining to paint an all-too-uncertain picture of the future. Add to that sudden expenses that can crop up—a child who is suddenly out of work, disability and accidents, evaporated retirement funds, or other unexpected costs. For those who have been forced into the unemployment sector, the potential or, worse, reality of such emergencies is alarming.

That can be especially distressing when you've enjoyed a steady income and schedule for decades. In fact, one of the most disconcerting elements of leaving the workplace is the sense that you're leaving behind your identity as well as your financial safety net. As Americans, we are consumed by our titles, work responsibilities, and career ambitions to such a degree that they become who we are during the course of our professional lives.

So it stands to reason that moving into a "retirement career" or new opportunity later in life won't occur without some trepidation—and should definitely not take place without considerable contemplation. Before doing anything, ask yourself this: *Is it wise to start another job or another career at this stage in my life? Or is staying put and making my current job more enticing the answer?*

A generation ago, older workers who weren't happy with their work situation likely endured misery in the name of reaching the retirement finish line, with their eyes on all the rewards that ten or twenty years of a relaxing post-work life could bring. These days, people aren't so eager to ride life out in such a passive manner, or aren't able to support a life that long without working full or part time—particularly when the period between a career and death spans decades, rather than a few years. Life expectancies are increasing, and extended time in the workplace means people sometimes need to be committed to what they're doing for a longer stretch. And if you're not enjoying your position, company, or profession, that can be a long, trying stretch.

Rather than resign themselves to jobs they are no longer enthused about as they were early in their careers, **older Americans are realizing that entire new careers can be built well beyond the age of fifty.** Of course, you have to be willing to make the commitment. And while many mature workers may want to explore professional alternatives, fewer people seem to have a defined vision for when exactly they'll leave the workplace or how. That may keep them working longer, or it may push them to find ways to transition out of the workplace gradually over time.

With any luck, your company has established a program to help you figure out which path is best for your career. At places like Ford Motor Company, where HR professionals are pushing for more employee-friendly work options, older workers aren't singled out for special work programs, but they are encouraged to participate in flex-time options that the company offers. The Transitional Work Arrangement, for example, allows employees to work a limited schedule—anywhere from 90 to 40 percent of their original workweek—with pay and benefits reduced accordingly. Ninety percent of the program's participants choose to work four-day weeks, says Rosalind Cox, the company's director of diversity, work life, and peer review. And though their pay and benefits drop along with their hours worked, the program allows older workers the opportunity to explore other options or ease out of the workload of their current jobs as they contemplate moving into retirement or another stage of their career.

Another option at Ford is the Alternative Work Schedule program, which allows staff to set up atypical work schedules, such as four ten-hour days, rather than a full, five-day workweek. Certain schedules, Cox says, have been adopted by entire departments, not just individual workers, because the firm has given managers much scheduling leeway. In addition, general flex-time programs allow workers to decide when they prefer to report for work—coming in and leaving later or earlier as needed.

The fact that a large corporation such as Ford is instituting programs like these hints that companies are realizing a greater need to help older staff members become more flexible later in their careers. But there's additional evidence to suggest that such programs are being implemented only slowly, despite the fact that they often cost companies very little. Human resource professionals seem widely aware of the impending shift in the nation's labor market. "Many of the conferences I've attended just in this past year had a huge focus on an older workforce," Cox says. But bringing that message to the very top tiers of a company can be a glacial process. At Ford, for example, Cox says, more and more attention is being focused on how to best strategize with older workers, but it's not a top priority among senior management. "I see [making the issue more urgent among senior leaders at Ford] as part of my responsibility so people are aware and start creating some strategy around that," Cox says.

She'll likely be joined in her push to bring this issue to the attention of executives by counterparts in other company offices. Corporate America is certainly waking to the fact that seniors retiring over the next several years are going to leave a massive gap in the country's labor pool. Organizations such as AARP are promoting such initiatives through programs like their yearly list of the AARP Best Employers for Workers Over 50. Likewise, HR consultancies like Watson Wyatt, and corporate management advocacy groups such as the Conference Board, survey and work with companies and employees to determine the needs of workers within American business and encourage companies to work toward those changes. But their efforts remain largely behind-the-scenes academic or industry-related work that is mentioned in business media, but not practiced widely throughout corporate offices.

And an ever-present attitude of *We'll cross that bridge when we come to it* may prevent some companies from taking a more proactive stance. As with the Y2K phenomenon, companies are treating the looming labor shortage crisis as another example of overhype. Even a giant corporation like IBM, which has created a special team to look at developing a "mature workers strategy," admits it has only begun to address the issue of an aging workforce.

Alternate Work Schedules

A 2003 study conducted by Watson Wyatt found that many workers left employers they'd spent an entire career with because they felt work-hour flexibility was limited—an increasing concern as older workers contemplate their careers and what they'd like to do next. Companies could do much to retain these workers with a few simple strategies created to meet employees' needs for the number of hours worked—strategies that employees could bring to the attention of their managers:

◆ **Phased Retirement.** Workers transition gradually into retirement or another career move by working fewer hours a day, week, or month and frequently reducing their level of responsibility as well. Phased retirement allows companies to hold on to valued workers for longer and allows individuals to ease work stresses and perhaps explore their next step professionally as they approach retirement.

◆ **Flex Time.** This option allows workers to create different times when they will come to work and leave, rather than sticking to a set schedule from, say, 8 AM to 5 PM.

◆ **Alternative Hours.** Employees create unusual work schedules, such as working ten days in a row and taking three or four days off, rather than working a traditional workweek.

◆ **Job Sharing.** Two or more employees share the same job position and alternate hours worked for that job so they each work fewer hours per week or day.

Should I Leave?

That this book focuses on people finding employment at ages fifty and beyond is telling in itself. Back when the dot-com bubble was churning out millionaires on paper by the dozens and much of corporate America dreamed of retirement at thirty, people began realizing how dramatically lives could shift—professionally and personally—from the trajectory typical a generation ago, when workers dutifully rode out their careers until retirement at sixty-five.

Many of the dot-com millionaires have been turned back into citizens with paltry bank accounts, their dreams of globe-trotting in retirement at thirty-five dashed. But if nothing else, the notion of people's work lives ending or at least shifting so early in their careers fueled ideas among older workers as well. Even for those whose bank accounts weren't swollen by skyrocketing stocks in the late 1990s, there was an idea brewing that careers could take on a whole new focus and meaning after, say, fifty. Most important, individuals didn't have to be committed to one career per lifetime—they could develop two, three, four careers, as many as they desired and had the time and means to pursue.

With that in mind, when to leave the workplace is probably the most important question on older workers' minds today, next to *Where should I go next?*

Plenty—some might argue a majority—of working Americans are uninspired by their jobs. According to Quintessential Careers, a careers Web site, **thirty million people go to work every day hating their job.** If you actually work the eleven thousand days that Quintessential Careers estimates you will during a lifetime, that's a lot of anguish to endure over a career.

If you feel that much resentment toward your employer or the work you do, it's a clue that exploring a new career option would be beneficial as you move into your later work years. But assessing your financial security, family support, commitment to change, and realistic future goals—as well as having an honest discussion with yourself about how you want to spend your later life professionally—are first on the list of things to do before you even consider leaving your current job, much less when or how to leave.

Saying good-bye to your current company or career, not to mention a daily routine, office camaraderie, and, ultimately, a huge part of personal identity can be little short of earth shattering. "In the past, if someone said, 'What do you do?' I would define myself as the vice president of XYZ company," says Robert Cannon, president of Cannon Advantage in Chagrin Falls, Ohio. "Now I see myself less as a piece of [corporate America] and more as an individual."

With that transition can come great personal and professional rewards. Indeed, the notion that a single career followed by a relaxing, comfortable retirement was the definition of success no longer holds true for a lot of people. (For many Americans, of course, that's still the key to success and fulfillment—and if that's true for you as well, don't try to alter your perception and chase another career simply because you think it's the new expected norm.) These days, the ability to strike out again, find a new passion later in life, and realize professional success in a new venture after fifty is quickly becoming the new definition of success—and a necessity for those who are suddenly jobless after fifty.

"There's this whole business of how to restructure, and many people start out by saying, 'Retirement is going to be so wonderful, because I can do what I want when I want,'" notes Millen of the Transition Network. But arriving at that next juncture can be daunting.

"At different points in time each of us comes to realize, that's not happening to me. Some realize in one and a half weeks and some realize in six years," Millen continues. In a regular questionnaire that she gives to new members, individuals are asked what their greatest concern is as they transition from their current workplace into the next phase of their life. Interacting with co-workers on a daily basis is always important. But of almost universal concern is workers' need for structure and their fear of its absence once they leave the office—something to consider when jumping from one job to the next.

Patricia Smith, vice president of New Directions, an organization in Boston that helps employees, usually fifty and older, assess the next stage of their life, including possible career or job changes and steps to getting there, recalls one client who at sixty-two announced to his company that he was going to retire. Except he couldn't bring himself to leave the office. So he continued to spend time at the company, infringing on his successor's ability to take over, as he pondered his next move through New Direction's program. Eventually he realized the burden he was placing on the person trying to fill his post and agreed to leave six months earlier than he had originally decided. "He was not letting go of his role," Smith says. "For many executives, this is their identity."

In a culture where the first question out of most people's mouths at cocktail parties, dinners—almost any social occasion—is "What do you do for a living?" it's disconcerting to suddenly have no response. Many people find themselves writing out daily, detailed to-do lists while between jobs, even if it's just a compilation of errands, exercise, phone calls, or other activities that seemingly wouldn't need strict deadlines. Plus, the financial stability of full-time work as well as the familiarity of the job you've come to know so well can be hard to turn your back on.

"I had access to a corporate jet. Now I have access to the family car. I've gone from putting the Four Seasons and Ritz-Carlton on the corporate tab to Marriott Courtyards and Days Inn on my own tab," Cannon says. "Do I miss it? No. I just see it as a difference." But the nuances of making a major career switch or leaving the workforce entirely weigh heavily on many people.

Phasing Out

An increasingly popular strategy for leaving a job is called phasing, in which workers leave the workplace in stages—often by reducing their responsibilities, assignments, and hours worked over months or years. It's a less shocking transition into retirement or a new line of work, say experts, for both employees and companies, which frequently tap phasers as mentors who can pass on their knowledge and skills to a younger generation as they're slowly exiting their careers.

In 1973, Fred Cook, previously a principal with Towers Perrin, started an executive compensation consultancy, which has since grown to a respected compensation firm that includes twenty-one people. "I just wanted to try working on my own and see if I could build a focused firm based on what I did, which was executive compensation consulting," Cook says.

Turns out he could. Now, thirty years later, Cook is ready to retire from his position as chairman of Frederic W. Cook and Company—sort of. "It's nice to step away gradually each year, although there's not anything particularly calling me, like fly fishing or golf."

So Cook, who is now sixty-three, plans to very gradually exit his office over the next ten years, reducing his hours from 5 to 20 percent each year. Doing so allows him to keep a hand in the business but with increasingly less responsibility and stress—and assures that he can continue to play a role in the firm's development and solidity years after he's stopped working. "My basic goal is to have the firm survive and prosper without me," says Cook, who is already grooming another company executive to take his place. Such a gradual departure is also far less jarring—for both Cook and his staff—than would be simply walking out on a Friday and being retired come Monday.

A similar approach is being adopted by workers in corporate America who don't want to be working one day, celebrate their retirement send-off, and be home trying to figure out what to do next the following week.

Experts caution that phased retirement is a slowly growing trend, evident in a few pioneering companies, and not a widespread phenomenon. But perhaps someday it will be. A 2003 Watson Wyatt study of a thousand workers over fifty reported that two-thirds would prefer to phase out of their current jobs. Companies would be wise to accommodate this desire as a way to hold on to vast numbers of boomers who might otherwise retire altogether, leaving a vast talent gap behind. Companies such as telecommunications firm Qualcomm Inc., in San Diego, and Ultratech Stepper, a manufacturer of semiconductor equipment in San Jose, California, are responding with phased-retirement programs to help workers transition into the next stage of their career or life. Telecommunications and the computer industry may, of course, be more open to some of these trends, because many employees have specific skills. Losing these workers would necessitate expensive training of younger staff or outside workers to fill those talent gaps. Still, phasing is just as beneficial to employees—a particularly ideal strategy for workers over fifty who are trying to figure out what job, career, or phase of their life they want to move into next.

Staffing firms like Boston's New Directions are recognizing the importance of older-worker trends such as phasing. They're targeting much of their business to working with executives, many of whom are fifty and above, who are still employed but want to consider a gradual exit strategy. Working with executives twelve to eighteen months before they depart, New Directions offers assessments consisting of everything from psychological screenings to career tests, analyzed by the staff's own psychologist.

One client, a CEO of a financial services firm, realized he relished being on the New York Stock Exchange floor, something he'd remembered and loved in his earlier career. Tapping into that memory and passion helped him make a career decision after years as an executive to become the head of the Boston stock exchange—certainly an upper-level job, but hardly one with the prestige of his CEO career. Arriving at that realization wasn't an overnight process, however. It required remaining in his current job and slowly phasing out through New Direction's self-examination process. "It took him three or four months to let go of [needing] to be a CEO, based on how other people perceive him or what he thought he needed to do to be successful," says Smith.

Indeed, letting go of prestige can be one of the hardest parts of leaving a job. Figuring out the next step is as much about planning your life as it is your next professional move. Making sweeping professional moves affects not only you but also your entire family. The transition can lead to surprises, from learning how you and your family feel about such moves to encountering unexpected possibilities that pop up as a result of exploration. According to Smith, 25 percent of New Directions clients leave the program with a career path or job they never before considered.

Advantages to Phased Retirement

◆ **Less Shock.** Transitioning out of the workplace in stages is far less disconcerting than simply exiting cold turkey one day after a decade or more at a company—not to mention thirty years or more of going to work every day. One of the most difficult things about retiring is not having an office, a social environment, or the sense of purpose that work so readily provides.

◆ **Time to Think.** Easing out of a current work situation, rather than quitting outright, gives older workers the chance to maintain an income and sense of stability and routine in their lives while exploring options.

◆ **An Ability to Lay Groundwork.** By phasing out, workers can discuss with their current employer future options such as part-time or consulting work as a former employee. They also have time to mentor a younger workforce coming up behind them.

Working on *Your* Time

If you're burned out by fifty-plus-hour workweeks over a twenty-five-year career, quitting cold turkey doesn't have to be your only option. And consider also that **many workers over fifty haven't adequately prepared for retirement, or have expenses that don't offer them the luxury of not working.** In addition, plenty of companies are offering flex- and part-time work hours, as well as telecommuting opportunities. Your company doesn't offer that kind of program? Don't count it out just yet. The majority of companies willing to let their workers fashion creative work schedules are starting to allow such practices to be worked out on a case-by-case basis between managers and individual employees. The key is knowing how to negotiate for such a work change. And more and more companies are now starting to foresee the mass exodus of boomers in the next ten years. Their concern about what such a labor shortage will mean to their workforce, productivity, and market performance bodes well for older workers trying to negotiate various work options. Negotiating flexible work schedules, alternative retirement departures, part-time work, and other work alternatives may thus be easier than in years past.

Cathy Fyock, who has researched and written widely about retirement strategies, cites an example of one information technology employee within a Lexington, Kentucky, hospital whose wife needed special medical care that she could only receive in Dallas. The worker, who had been a reliable, highly valued employee since he was hired in his fifties, was now seventy, and feeling compelled to walk away from his job entirely to be with his wife. Instead, his supervisor—who is convinced the older workers in her department are a key to its success—negotiated a special work schedule whereby the man could work every other month, allowing him to keep his job and salary but still be with his wife frequently. Other companies offer similar or equally progressive programs.

A Sampling of Companies Courting the Older Worker

♦ **Scripps Health**, San Diego, California. At Scripps, any employee can participate in the organization's job-sharing program, but it seems particularly suitable for older employees. Through the program, two employees share a single job and maintain their skills but work far fewer hours per week. The group also offers flex-time programs, compressed workweek schedules, and telecommuting options for workers; it even goes so far as to offer support such as home office equipment and skills training. Through the company's Career Transition Program (CTP), a retention and recruitment initiative, employees can receive pay and benefits for three months while they look for possible jobs inside or outside the organization.

◆ **Loudoun Healthcare Inc.**, Leesburg, Virginia. The organization partnered with George Mason University in Arlington, Virginia, to offer classes on site at Loudon allowing employees to pursue further degrees through a tuition forgiveness program. Experts predict that more companies will employ such programs in the future, when skilled workers retire and businesses are left with a younger, less skilled workforce that needs to be brought up to speed as quickly as possible.

◆ **Hoffmann-La Roche Inc.**, Nutley, New Jersey, offers an on site placement agency that helps place former and retired employees in temporary positions.

◆ **St. Mary's Medical Center**, Huntington, West Virginia. Like Hoffmann, St. Mary's offers a reentry program whereby former nurses can be placed in available positions, but the hospital's program also includes flexible work schedules and is specifically oriented toward the lifestyles of retired employees.

Source: AARP 2004 Best Employers for Workers Over 50.

Explore Before Moving On

If you feel your company no longer values you, or your employer expects staff to depart at a certain age, that looming deadline can be stressful, particularly if your finances aren't in order. Too many workers have been blindsided by unexpected investment losses in recent years, forcing them to work longer. How long they can hang on may be frightening if their company expects, or even requires, them to leave at a certain age.

Take the case of United Airlines. In the summer of 2004, the company said in bankruptcy court that it would terminate its pension contributions and replace them with defined contribution plans, similar to 401(k) retirement programs. This decision affects all United employees, including flight attendants, mechanics, and gate agents. It also has an immense impact on pilots, who are required by the Federal Aviation Administration to retire at sixty. That's an age far short of today's life expectancies. What are retired pilots to do when their pension has been terminated or severely restricted? It's a scary question, but as the following story reveals, one that can be resolved.

A required departure was an increasing concern for one older worker. For twenty years, Christine Millen was a partner at Deloitte Consulting working with behemoths like the United Nations and Merrill Lynch. "It was always on a very large scale, and it was fabulous," Millen says. Except for one sticking point: Deloitte required that all partners retire at sixty-two. With that mandate looming, somewhere in her midfifties—and more so after her mother died—Millen began thinking, "At what point do I build a different life? I decided I wanted to build one well before sixty."

So Millen did what any stressed older worker might do: She asked questions. Lots of questions. "I had a good friend with a senior job at the UN," Millen says. "She teases me now and says, 'You used to keep taking me out to lunch and ask, *What do you do in the morning and the following day? And then the morning after that?*' I couldn't figure out what people did next or how it worked. How did you make friends? How did you approach organizations where you wanted to work? What if you promised to do work and then you didn't like it?"

The prospect of what lay beyond her current workplace felt amorphous and daunting for Millen. "As I wrestled with this, I realized it's a black box. I don't know anything about this world [of working during retirement], and very few other women knew about it." Then she hit upon an idea. She wanted to work, but not within the confines of the daily grind she'd thrived on for two decades. Fortunately for Millen, Deloitte was willing to negotiate alternatives to her current schedule. So, starting in 2000, Millen began working on a project basis—taking on assignments for two years at a stretch, at times, then taking three or four months off.

"I knew I wanted to work less, but I didn't want to work three days a week, because I wanted big chunks of time to myself." Millen also knew that if she didn't work full time for those two years, she would be relegated to less engaging assignments. "It had to be challenging and all-consuming, otherwise it wasn't any fun."

What Millen negotiated with Deloitte was an early version of phased retirement. And while she explored that ground without much help, many companies have since developed similar offerings, some in formalized programs. Deloitte actually created a Senior Leaders program around the same time as Millen's project work began, though the program has since been eliminated after a change in corporate structure.

Other workers would be wise to follow Millen's lead—examining their own options, skills, and interests as well as what the world offers outside the professional life they've become accustomed to. For example, if you're examining a new career, you'll do better if you find out not only what jobs are currently available in that field, but also where those jobs could take you, as well as other potential career paths in your new line of interest.

The key to making a smooth transition, of course, is having plenty of time to investigate your options and make a plan. Too many people heading into retirement or a new professional venture take the plunge with little more than a vague notion of how they plan to spend the next ten to fifteen years—or whether that move is even the right thing for them at the moment. Despite recent trends toward considering various work and volunteer alternatives to retirement, a great number of people follow the behavior patterns of their parents and either head into the same retirement role at the same age, or fail to consider the fact that other options exist until they are on the brink of exiting their careers.

Millen's self-exploration wasn't without its frustrations: soul searching, tireless digging for answers, and discovering that some plans simply won't work. But her exhaustive efforts were worth it given her new post-retirement existence. And such self-exploration isn't a bad strategy for other workers looking to ease out of their current work situation.

Identify Your Biggest Motivators

- What turns you on about your job?
- What did you hate about it?
- Think about your really good days and really bad days. What made them that way?

Research New Interests Now

- Always wanted to take Spanish or work for a non-profit? Great: Do it *before* you leave your job. That way you won't be afraid to hate it or feel obligated to stick it out.
- Looking into interests during your current job also gives you a steady cash flow while doing so. Burning through savings to explore possible interests after leaving your job

will add to your stress, possibly killing your optimism for a field that might otherwise spark your interest.

Jump in ASAP

♦ If your plan is to volunteer after leaving the workplace, do so now, since some organizations may have training programs or waiting periods before you can enter their programs. The same approach holds true for new job opportunities—start exploring them in your current position so you have a head start when you do actually leave your current career.

Don't Be Afraid to Fail

♦ It's an old, overworn saying but it's been repeated ad nauseum because it's true: If you can't face the possibility of failure, then your best bet is to sit tight where you are.

♦ And if you do fail? Put that other age-old adage to work and learn from your mistakes.

Make an Exit Plan

So you've decided to leave your current work situation. Good for you. Now stop. Don't just quit cold turkey. For starters, you could throw your life into a tailspin, take on incredible stress financially and emotionally, and ultimately put yourself right back where you started if quitting suddenly is so terrifying that you run back to a similar job for the sake of security.

You may be miserable at your current place of employment

and loathe each second of your daily commute to the office. On the other hand, you've already got a steady paycheck, a benefits package, and the safety of knowing that you're supported while you look around for something else. It seems like common sense, but plenty of people near retirement, eager to get out of their daily grind, get caught up in the excitement of new opportunities, environments, and the ability to leave their old job behind and chuck it all before they should.

Instead, explore options while you're still employed—negotiate a reduction in hours or responsibilities if that's what it takes—like opening your own business, switching careers, finding a similar job within a different industry, or going back to school. If nothing else, now is the time to kick-start your network of contacts for job leads, start researching other companies and industries, update your résumé, and begin considering your professional strengths and skills and where they can take you, among other things, before kicking your current job to the curb.

If your ideas about your next move remain murky, it's particularly important to explore options while you're still pulling in a paycheck. If, for example, you're a sales manager but always wanted to be a landscape architect, take a class on the subject now to see if structuring flower beds and pruning rosebushes is really all that you've imagined it to be. You may realize that hands-on work outdoors, under the sun for eight hours at a stretch, is a liberation—or that it's backbreaking labor leaving you pining for your air-conditioned cubicle.

Start researching your dream career or business while you still have a job. It will make exploring that much less nerve racking, give you time to really consider your next move, and likely provide a stress release from your daily routine.

Draw up a specific time line for your next move with mini

weekly and monthly deadlines along the way. Don't worry if you don't meet every one of those deadlines exactly—the idea is to give yourself a general time frame for when you'd like to leave your current job. Reaching your goal may require multiple changes along the way—don't add stress to your life by hanging the time line over your head as if it's a quarterly sales quota that has to be met.

Once you do decide to head out the door, make sure you do so professionally. Even at the end of your career, when you think you may no longer need all those professional contacts as you head into a new line of work, it's smart to assume that the world is a very small place. You never know when you may run into former colleagues again—or need to use them as references or professional contacts.

Dr. Randall Hansen, head of online job board and career advice site Quintessential Careers, offers the following advice for exiting your current place of employment gracefully:

◆ **Give Plenty of Notice.** It's typical to give at least two weeks' notice when leaving—and sometimes more. Ask your supervisor what he thinks is best, or consult your employee handbook for official company rules on giving notice.

◆ **Negotiate Pay.** Don't leave without all the outstanding pay due you—vacation, sick and personal days, commission payments, outstanding salary, and other compensation. Doing so after your departure can become a difficult, messy ordeal.

◆ **Fill Your Shoes.** Want to make your employer's life easier? Offer to help find a replacement for the position you're vacating, then offer to train that replacement before you leave.

♦ **Don't Coast.** It's a common phenomenon among exiting workers—coasting through their last days as they bide their time before leaving. Do that and, no matter how hard you've worked for the past ten years, your boss is likely to remember how you shirked your duties on your way out. Instead, make sure you complete all your assignments in a timely and professional manner, just as you've (hopefully) done during the rest of your tenure at the company. And make sure you update your boss and peers on where your projects stand.

♦ **Leave on a Positive Note.** Don't get caught up in company naysayers who may see a departing employee as an ally in negativity. You don't want to leave on a bad note.

♦ **One Last Good-Bye.** On your last day, reconnect with your supervisors, get their contact information, and thank them once more for all their support and help. As the saying goes, you never want to burn your bridges. Even later in life, when you think contacts may be increasingly less important because your career is winding down, you never know when an old colleague could start you off on a new career path.

Stay Put and Change

Maybe exiting isn't the solution. For those laid off, the decision has already been made. But for many workers, a new lease on work is not about changing a career entirely, but simply breathing new life into the one they've already got. And for valued employees who have committed years of effort to their company, managers will likely be open to working alternatives. In fact, some of the best working arrangements are orchestrated between supervisor and employee rather than through overarching company programs.

If you haven't done so already, approach your boss and be honest—albeit in a positive, productive manner—about why you want to examine alternate work schedules. Perhaps you'd like to spend more time working on some family issues; maybe your job isn't inspiring to you at the moment; you might not be feeling overwhelmingly tied to your career currently; or perhaps you'd like to lessen your workload over the next five years as you refocus and figure out how you can better reengage with your workplace. Or, if you need to infuse new life into your same position, maybe changing your responsibilities, rather than taking on more, is the boost you need.

No matter what, there are a few things to keep in mind when negotiating a new role at your current job:

◆ **Be Flexible.** You may have put in your time as a loyal, hard-charging, fifteen-year employee, but taking a gentler, kinder approach is more likely to land you a new self-carved role. Be willing to work odd hours or help in areas where you're not usually needed.

◆ **Make Your Case.** You've worked at the company for years. Surely you've picked up some invaluable skills that could be transferred to a more scintillating role. Highlight those skills and how they could be enhanced, altered, or—with just a little bit of training—transformed to open up a whole new area of potential for your company or department.

◆ **Write It Out.** Chances are, if your boss is as busy as the rest of corporate America, the last thing she wants dropped on her agenda is the task of writing a new job description for the new position you're suggesting. Make her life easy—write out a job description ahead of time, along with the benefits the new position could bring to your company, such as department improvements, market advantages, increased revenue, and other returns. Include specific numbers, statistics, or other concrete information that will help drive home your case.

◆ **Clean Up Behind Yourself.** Your company may be more apt to approve a major change in responsibilities if you can account for who will fill in the gaps and pick up where your old responsibilities left off. Suggest people who can fill your role, departmental shifts that could close the gaps in your absence, or other means to help fill the void that your move on may leave behind.

Chapter 3

A New Career, A New Start

In an age of fear—fear of being laid off, of having too little money to retire on, of impending terrorist attacks, of the economy taking a nosedive—it stands to reason that many workers would seek out more security and less change and simply stay put in their current jobs. Why up the fear factor by venturing into a new job or, worse, a new career?

Well, because plenty of people are finding that what could have simply been their leisurely retirement years are instead a chance to finally dive into the career they always wanted. Others who never planned on career change are seeing an opportunity pass before them and seizing it.

Jack Johnston, a former SeaWorld vice president of marketing, was unexpectedly laid off with 125 other employees during a serious lull in tourism during the 1990s. He had no idea what he would do next. What he finally ended up pursuing as a profession was as shocking to him as anyone.

At the time he had six children, one with leukemia, and had blown through his savings paying for medical expenses to fight his child's cancer. "I was all of a sudden broke and having a very, very difficult time," says Johnston, whose wife had also been laid off. For some reason, when he thought about what to do next, he kept returning to his love of art. Around Christmas that year Johnston's wife was admiring a fifteen-hundred dollar Santa Claus doll, well beyond Johnston's Christmas budget. There was no way he could afford it, so he decided to make one instead, using clay from his local craft store. Surprisingly, "it came out very well," Johnston says. "I thought, *What's the potential of marketing this piece?*" He soon found out. For forty-five dollars, he rented a vendor table at a local craft show and set up his one doll. The vendor next to him, whose table was full of handcrafted dolls, took one look at Johnston's single item and asked how much. He hadn't even thought about it. "How much are you selling yours for?" he replied. Hers were $129 each. It seemed like a fair price, so he agreed to sell his for the same. She bought Johnston's doll on the spot. "I realized that if a competitor would buy it at that price, I had some-thing," Johnston says. He took orders for eight dolls that first day. Then he slowly started raising the price—first to $299, then moving his way up to as high as $1,000 per doll for some of his creations. "I made 218 one-of-a-kind dolls that first year," he says. "A business was born."

It certainly was. Since then, Johnston has built his doll-making business by writing a book on how to craft dolls, creating a series of eight videos and four DVDs that sell for $49.95 apiece, and developing a lecture series that takes him on a tour of forty-two cities in the United States and Europe each year, in addition to the creation of ProSculpt, a new form of clay used by many of his peers within the industry. Today Johnston's business pulls in four million dollars a year; he's been featured on PBS specials and within the pages of *Better Homes & Gardens* magazine.

Johnston found a hidden talent and exploited it to launch a thriving business, by creatively adding lectures, products, and services that he knew the market needed. Not everyone may have such an unusual talent to tap into, but most of us have unseen skills and abilities that we've either squandered earlier in our careers, or simply never fully recognized and developed. Now is the time to focus on what those may be and how they could offer a new working opportunity.

If you want to completely overhaul your working situation, the best way of doing so is by transferring a skill you already have to another profession. And often the best way to do that is to figure out your greatest talents in your current position. Think back on projects at work where you had great success:

- ◆ What made those projects more successful than others you handled?
- ◆ What tasks give you the most energy and comfort on the job? Those may be an indicator of natural talents that could be developed further.
- ◆ Which of those talents that you use regularly could propel you into another career?
- ◆ When has your interest been particularly sparked at work?
- ◆ What was it about that assignment that piqued your curiosity and made you more inspired?
- ◆ How could you transfer that inspiration to another line of work?
- ◆ What talents have your peers taken notice of or complimented you on?
- ◆ What skills and assets that you bring to the company are regularly acknowledged and praised during your employee reviews?

◆ Think about colleagues who might have already made the leap. How did they transfer their skill sets to another position or company?

Time and again, it seems workers who find their true professional calling later in life do so by recognizing what really excites them and then exploiting that in a very strategic manner.

As a kid, Steven Smith always wanted to be in law enforcement. But as a "nice Jewish boy" growing up in the Northeast, he was always told that the law enforcement line of work "is not for you. You're going to go into business and do something more entrepreneurial."

So he did. For more than twenty years, Smith ignored his early passion for law enforcement and held high-level positions, mainly within software companies, where he learned much about software and technology strategy and planning. When the dot-com market bottomed out in early 2001, Smith, by chance, was offered a chance to work briefly in the local sheriff's department. It might be interesting, he thought, but he soon left, because what he thought would be "police work" turned out to be technical oversight of the local jails, not the vision of law enforcement work he had imagined.

Still, it laid a foundation on which Smith could build to gain entrée into his local police department, which he was able to do shortly after. How? He identified a key weakness in the bureau that he knew the department's chief agreed was of concern: a lack of technological sophistication. This dovetailed perfectly with Smith's background.

He managed to work his way into the police force by offering to work one day a week to help create a technology bureau that the chief of police saw as crucial to more advanced law enforcement practices within his department. Gradually, over time, that one day a week led to full-time employment within the police department for Smith—something he'd been coveting for years.

Smith's position, which is administrative, not on the streets, may not be the police job he envisioned as a child, but it puts him in the environment he always dreamed of working in. "You have a childhood dream to be a policeman, but at fifty-five, you're not going to the academy, so what's the next best thing?"

The next best thing took "six years of hard labor," as Smith puts it, "volunteering, doing part-time employment," proving that he had a talent the department hadn't yet capitalized on. His efforts paid off. "Do I have a gun, a radio, and a car? No," Smith admits. "But am I helping them to work smarter by implementing digital images and technology? Absolutely. I'm looking to build a legacy that I can be proud of."

It's important to remain flexible and open to all sorts of job possibilities when changing careers. When Smith was a child, his vision of law enforcement was donning a police uniform and fighting crime on the streets. But after a certain age, that's no longer a viable option. Rather than hang up his dream, though, Smith remained open to other roles he could play within the department. Ultimately, it got him to the same spot, albeit in a slightly different function.

Making the Leap

It also pays to be open to different segments of the business market. If you spent your career in pharmaceutical sales and now you want to be in marketing, it doesn't mean that you have to stick to a corporate giant, although you also have to know your limitations on salary shifts. There are plenty of opportunities in the nonprofit world that provide rich work environments and personal rewards that profit-based firms don't always deliver. And smaller firms are frequently more likely to take a chance on someone with less experience than a corporate giant where top candidates in their field—from executives to the assembly floor—are knocking on the door every day looking for work.

Gerry Beauchamp had seen a lot of change in five years. As the vice president of human resources for John Hancock Signature Services in Boston, he had built the company's staff in burgeoning markets to thirteen hundred employees. Then just as quickly he had to decrease it again. The economy had tanked, newly opened business units were closed after a year or two of operations, and people were being let go by the hundreds. When it was all done, John Hancock's staff had been whittled back down to nine hundred and Beauchamp was feeling frayed, exhausted, and demoralized by the events. That's when he was offered a promotion as director of HR within the company's corporate structure.

Beauchamp stopped to consider all that was at stake. His daily commute was an hour-plus each way—on good days—from his home in Ipswich on Boston's North Shore to the company's downtown office building. (The perk of free parking for executives was beginning to lose its luster.) He really liked the people he worked with, but professionally he didn't envision a better, more inspiring place for himself at his current company. He'd been worn down during the economic tailspin over the past two years. And most of all, "I had a son at the time who was a sophomore in high school and not doing well," Beauchamp says. "I wanted to spend more time closer to home.

This was also post–9/11 and I found myself saying, 'If I can do something close to home, for less money, but get more involved in the community, I'd do it.'"

At the time, Beauchamp recalls, he was so entrenched in the happenings of downtown Boston—where his office was—that on weekends, he and his wife would walk through his local township and neighbors would say hello to his wife and hardly recognize him. It was upsetting, he says.

So without a job in hand, Beauchamp, then fifty-three, negotiated an early-retirement package and walked away in January 2002 from a fifteen-year stint as an HR executive to forge a new career that would bring him closer to home. By May, he was the new executive director of the Ipswich YMCA. In a facility just two years old, the current executive director was leaving; two friends who had been involved in the facility's original development asked Beauchamp if he'd like the job. Beauchamp said no. But two weeks later, during the first hour of a fifteen-mile run, they approached him again, spent an hour persuading him to reconsider, and finally managed to pique Beauchamp's interest. "I was intrigued because it was presented as a business with over a hundred employees where only six worked full time."

And it was struggling. The notion of handling the Y more like a business, and less like a nonprofit entity, made the job more appealing to Beauchamp. "They needed someone to come in and demonstrate a different leadership and management strategy," he says.

Since then, he's vastly expanded the Y's facilities, programs, and services. He introduced half a dozen special events for the community, created a triathlon and holiday runs for local residents, established camps for kids during the summer, and built a baseball and soccer field and ropes course. Currently he's helping to lead a ten-million-dollar public housing effort funded by the state, but largely driven by the YMCA. "My salary has declined 50 percent and I miss John Hancock every two weeks when I get paid," Beauchamp jokes. "But I'm still happy with my choice."

A drastic career move later in life is really about testing your values, Beauchamp believes. **You have to ask yourself: What really motivates me, my paycheck or happiness with my job every day?** The two can go hand in hand, of course, but that's not always the case. And there's no shame in saying that money is your number one motivator, even if it means loathing the job you're in. Honesty about what turns you on is really the key. "Are you true to yourself? I had a respectable nest egg. Now I'm nervous," Beauchamp admits. "We don't have much debt but I have two kids in college. That's fifty-six thousand dollars a year. I have only a modest pension that will start this year. But factoring all of that in, I'm still happy with the choice I made. I never worry about whether or not I did the wrong thing."

Thousands of fifty-plus employees like Beauchamp, demoralized, uninspired, and frazzled, have been spit out by corporate America in recent years—the result of market shifts, corporate downsizings, bonus cuts, and rigid management, which lost its flexibility with employees long ago when the economy went sour, driving individuals away.

Time to Go?

Like Beauchamp, if you find yourself bored with your daily tasks, dreading company meetings and trips, or watching the clock for the first time in a twenty-year career, it could well be time to move on—even to an entirely new profession. But make sure it is, first.

Seeking out a new career requires very careful consideration, assessment, and, most of all, time. Never rush a process as important as changing a career, especially if you already have a job and have the luxury of a steady paycheck and benefits.

Starting a new career at any age is daunting. Sure, it happens. There are certainly people who have started law school in their forties or attended medical school in their thirties or even as late as forty. Doing so after fifty, of course, is an altogether different endeavor. That said, however, the truth is, almost anything can be accomplished if you want it badly enough. And that's the key: really wanting it. If you've always had a passing interest in photography and think kicking your lofty six-figure CFO job to the curb for a shot at becoming a photojournalist sounds romantic, it is. But be prepared to see your salary drop to five figures—on the low end—and assume that you have to start at the bottom. You may find yourself shooting the local pet show or shots for a feature on the weather in which you catch a family at play on a windy day. Not exactly the excitement of a war zone—or even a local political campaign.

That said, if you still want to take the plunge, the rewards of pursuing a career you've always coveted can be immense.

First Things First

If you really want to pursue a new career, know exactly what sacrifices you're willing to make to see that dream happen. Not willing to travel every month? Then a career in sales, for example, probably isn't for you.

You might start by asking yourself a few questions and delving within for truly honest answers:

◆ **Why Do I Want to Pursue This Career?** Be honest here. If it's about glamour, prestige, or proving your professional worth, tread very cautiously. Few jobs ever deliver on those goals with ease.

It's no secret that being successful at any occupation takes long hours of slogging through hard work. But observing a profession from the outside can make it appear easier and more glamorous than it actually is. Take the case of one doctor who was intent on breaking into the advertising business. He called an advertising recruitment firm in New York and expressed his disgust with a lot of today's print and television advertising, describing it as dull, uninspired, and exceedingly unimaginative. Surely he could write better copy himself, he said, and offered up his experience writing medical reports as evidence of his copy-writing skills.

What the recruiter suggested was that he focus, at least for the moment, on writing copy for medical ads, as a way to transition into the industry. But this arrogant doctor had his sights set more on reworking Budweiser's latest campaign and was too proud to start within a less glamorous area of the industry. Perhaps he wasn't really as impassioned about advertising as he thought if he wasn't willing to work his way from the ground up.

◆ **Am I Willing to Start at the Bottom?** Your chances of landing your ideal job—or even the fifth on your list—aren't great in your first foray into a new field. In fact, you may have to consider entry-level positions. Have you read *Vanity Fair* for years and always thought it would be cool and exciting to write about celebrities, scandal, gossip, and the year's best Oscar parties? It probably would be, but with little to no experience doing so, your best possible job at a publication like that is probably as a fact checker, if that—a position that can pay as little as twenty-two thousand a year.

In almost any career, moving up the ladder can happen quickly if you're willing to work hard, show your commitment, and make sacrifices for the sake of your career. But if that's not going to dovetail with your current lifestyle or you don't think you have the energy, then you may want to reconsider whether or not a new career is for you—or at least think of a career where your current skills could more easily transfer you to a midlevel position.

◆ **How Much Time and Money Am I Willing to Spend on My Goal?** If you don't have alternate income, savings, or a family whose income can support you while you're chasing this particular career dream, it may be unrealistic. Embarking on a whole new career can require an additional degree, depending on what it is you're interested in doing—and one degree could wipe out a huge portion of a nest egg. Plenty of new careers don't require going back to school, but they will demand hours of time getting up to speed on your new industry or profession. If you've got young children or other life commitments, are you willing to sacrifice time with them to achieve your ultimate professional goal?

◆ **Will I Have a Problem Taking Orders from Someone Younger than Me?** If you change careers later in life, don't be surprised if your boss is ten or more years younger than you, especially if it's an industry filled with a lot of youthful workers. Of course, your supervisor might learn a great deal from you as well, simply given your longer time in the workforce, but be prepared to cast aside any issues you may have about following the leadership of someone who could be half your age. If you don't think an attitude adjustment is in your future when it comes to working with the younger set, walk away now and save yourself a lot of professional anguish.

◆ **Can I Give Up the Perks of a Former Job?** If you've spent an entire career in one industry, position, or company, chances are you've acquired some amenities along the way—a cherished company parking spot, corner office with a window, first-class travel privileges. Change careers and all of that will most likely vanish overnight. Of course, if you're more inspired and motivated by your new profession, none of that will matter. But plenty of people who think they want a new career don't stop to think about everything they'll be giving up to get there.

◆ **Can I Move?** Are you willing to even consider the option? If not, you could wildly reduce your chances of finding a job in your new occupation. Moving later in life can be a stressful venture, especially if you've spent years cultivating friendships, developing community relationships, and otherwise rooting yourself in your city's surroundings. But the reality is that plenty of older workers have failed to find success in a new field because they weren't willing to relocate. If you live in a city where the industry you're interested in offers only one or two potential employers, you might want to rethink your willingness to relocate—or to pursue that given career.

Making It Easy

Aside from making a career transition easier by transferring a skill from one profession to another, making the move to a whole new career can be easier when knocking on the doors of industries that are eager to hire. Certain fields, such as technology, health care, and education, are starting to feel or have been feeling a talent crunch for some time. But first you have to know which industry doors you even want to knock on. Then you have to have a plan for doing so.

It's key for everyone making a huge life transition to get family and friends behind them. Never is this more true than for older workers. You need to consider how your career change might affect finances, time, emotional support, and stress levels within a household. **Now is not the time to go it alone.** Sit down with your family and talk to them about why you want to change careers, what support you'll need from them, and what kind of changes they can expect—being gone interviewing for jobs, earning a smaller salary, being overwhelmed by new responsibilities—as your career changes.

Of course, letting your neighbors, friends, and colleagues in on your plan to refocus your professional ambitions can do much to bring extra support, advice, and—hopefully—contacts that can help you get a head start on your new occupation. One word of caution: Not everyone may have your best interests at heart. Be wary of naysayers, negative influencers, and people who simply aren't comfortable with change. They'll likely try to discourage you from your goals. While it's key to enlist family and friends for moral support, avoid those likely to bring you down in your search for greater professional gain.

Finding a New Direction

So now that you're committed to making a change, you need a plan—and a rock-solid one at that. Where to begin? Start with the following:

◆ **What's Great and Awful About Your Current Job?** Make a list of pros and cons, if necessary, but write down everything you love and hate about your current position. What's great about your co-workers? Do you like the hours? Is the cubicle environment something you want to duplicate or eliminate in your next job? Do you have enough autonomy, or is being closely guided a comfort in your everyday work habits? What skills do you have now that you could transfer to a new profession? We often work for years and never stop to think much about the specific, even minute details within our daily work lives that turn us on and off. Now's your opportunity to get rid of the ones that drive you crazy.

◆ **Refine the List.** Now that you've got a list, categorize it, listing the items—from most important to least—that make you happy at work. If there are things not a part of your current work situation that you'd like to include in the next go-round, such as working outdoors, start writing those down now. You may not get them all, but at least you'll start to realize what type of work and work environment you should really be pursuing. And you may start to notice patterns appear again and again.

◆ **Get External Feedback.** You've made some initial lists, and had a couple of honest, in-depth conversations with your inner professional. Now it's time to juxtapose your own perceptions against those of the people who might have a more objective viewpoint about yourself. Co-workers, friends, and family are definitely wise choices. But don't forget any company mentors, professional contacts, or others you would feel comfortable talking to who may not work with you on a regular basis, but have been regular fixtures in your professional life. As objective observers, they may have surprisingly poignant insights into your strengths and weaknesses. And when it comes to weaknesses, don't be afraid to ask others for constructive criticism. The key is to take it for what it is—productive commentary, not insults that could set you back in your search for a new line of work.

◆ **Seek Outside Help.** It might pay off to seek the services of a career coach. There are loads of them specializing in various professions and levels of employment. The Professional Association of Résumé Writers & Career Coaches offers a search engine on its Web site (www.parw.com) for professionals who can help with writing résumés, interviewing, career counseling, and other needs. If you simply want to explore without investing dollars and time, there are many free personality and professional tests online that you can find through a simple search on Google and other search engines.

◆ **Go Straight to the Source.** If you want to find out about a particular career, start talking to those who are already employed in the kinds of jobs you want. Set up informational interviews—they're one of the best ways to learn about the nuances, daily responsibilities, pros and cons, and opportunities within a particular field. Plus, you increase your chances of adding contacts within that industry or profession substantially if you make a favorable impression. But don't wait for your one contact to refer you on. If you feel a good rapport has been established during the course of a conversation, ask your interviewer if she would be willing to refer you to three more contacts she knows. And don't forget to ask her for names of professional organizations that might be of help.

The Job-Search Basics

For many workers over fifty who have been in a job for a long time or spent years in a company moving up through a series of positions, writing a cover letter, assembling a résumé, and going on interviews can be long-forgotten, now foreign experiences. Those who were recently let go from their jobs can suddenly be faced with drafting such materials from scratch (with former résumés long since tossed out while a former career was thriving) and preparing for interviews that they haven't been through for ten or twenty years. That's a burdensome task, but it doesn't have to be. Below, a few quick cover letter and résumé rules to consider.

Cover Letters

◆ **Make a Contact.** Always address the letter to a single individual, never "to whom it may concern" or a generic post, like "HR Department," even though a human resource professional will most likely be inspecting your résumé. If there is no name listed with the job posting, try to call the company and get one.

◆ **Get to the Point.** Your cover letter is an opportunity to effectively grab someone's attention—and fast. It's not the time to be long-winded about your many years of experience or to try to impress someone with your mastery of four-syllable words. Start off with a short introduction of yourself and keep your letter to a few quick introductory sentences or short paragraphs in simple language. Bullet points are an effective way to draw a recruiter's attention directly to your main points, strengths, or whatever you feel is necessary to highlight.

Never make the cover letter more than one page, **especially when sending by e-mail. Employers and recruiters simply don't have the time or inclination to read such lengthy pieces of correspondence.**

◆ **Read Carefully.** Examine the job posting carefully then use your cover letter to quickly and simply respond to the needs it mentions, succinctly explaining why you'd be great for the job based upon these needs. Recruiters and employers want to know that your skills will dovetail nicely with the position's requirements. Ramble on about general skills that don't match the job listing and you could quickly find your cover letter in the reject pile.

◆ **Follow Up.** Unless the job posting specifically states "no phone calls," show initiative and say you will follow up on a specific date to see when an interview might be scheduled— then make sure you actually call on that date specified. It's not overzealous to follow up two weeks after that. You don't want to overdo it, but supervisors remember people who are persistent.

Résumés

♦ **Keep It Recent.** It's a good idea to limit your list of work experience to the last fifteen years. Age discrimination is rampant enough, so don't make it any easier than you have to for employers to guess your age by gauging your time in the labor market. It may seem unfair to work twenty-five years and not acknowledge all of those efforts on your résumé, but the reality is that doing so alerts employers to your age and may foster a feeling that your skills are rooted in archaic practices—even though they're not.

♦ **Tout Current Skills.** Even if you leave off your first dozen years of work, your age may still be apparent. So play up recent skills, along with classes taken and certifications gained in the past few years. Skip listing the bachelor's degree you got in 1950 (or if you do mention it, leave off the year you graduated); emphasize instead the series of computer classes you took a year ago.

♦ **Keep It Short, Organized, and to the Point.** Highlight—in a chart if need be—your skills, past work experience, and other accomplishments. A more rambling, narrative résumé can be a laborious exercise in reading even for those just starting out with little work experience. For a seasoned, midlevel manager with years of employment under his belt, a three-page résumé with lengthy, cumbersome paragraphs is the last thing a recruiter or human resource manager wants to peruse.

♦ **Back It Up with Numbers.** Don't just say you were a highly valued employee; back it up by specifically stating that you got a promotion, for example, within six months of joining your department. Or if you're in sales, state your sales or percentage over quota for the last year or quarter. It always has a greater impact to read numbers than generalities.

Human resource professionals, career coaches, and recruiters remain divided over how many résumés an individual needs. Some feel that older workers, who may have a host of different skills they've picked up over the course of a career, might be better off subdividing those talents among a series of résumés they can tweak for various job postings. Others think one comprehensive résumé is enough.

Regardless, all agree on one thing: Any résumé submitted should be concise and easy to scan. What follows is a résumé in two versions—before and after, if you will. The original résumé is full of information. The problem is that employers have to either read the whole résumé for the few bits of information they're looking for—not ideal for those trying to move the hiring process along quickly—or try to jump in somewhere and randomly hunt and peck for key details.

The second résumé makes that process much simpler. The chart format makes reading and pinpointing key facts and work history far easier than a narrative résumé. And important bits of information, such as recent skill sets and when they were last used, jump off the page for quick access by HR professionals. Make reading your résumé a little more difficult, and interviewers are just as likely to chuck it in the trash as they are to toss it in the list of applicants to be interviewed—particularly if your résumé is number 237 in the pile of those to be reviewed.

Original Résumé

Marie Jones
1515 Elm Street
New York, NY 55555
Home: 222-222-2222
Cell: 222-222-1111

Objective: To give 100 percent and by so doing improve the sales and profitability of the company. As a team player I will increase client retention, maximize sales, and analyze the current market situation to best position the company's products. I will manage my team and develop their skills to ensure they become successful and teach them how to develop close relationships with their clients by offering them the very best customer service and advice. In this way we will always be first on the client's buy list.

Work History:

ABC Company, New York, NY—VP, Sales and Marketing
4/2001–present

I currently develop strategic alliances, find new clients for their marketing services, and deal with PR/marketing issues including Web site development. I researched and implemented a software billing solution to help bring the A/R back within industry norms. The principal within ABC Co. also co-owns a record label called ABC Records of which I am VP for marketing and PR. I negotiate with new acts and advise on many of their marketing issues, issue press releases, and have developed a music news editorial database.

DEF Company Inc. New York, NY—Advertising Director
7/1996–3/2001

Managed and sold the advertising for various magazines. Developed lasting relationships with many Fortune 1000 clients in the software, high tech, and music industries (many of which were software companies). Built up the worldwide client base by 30 percent and helped launch XYZ magazine (Abe Carter's first venture into consumer magazines). Increased revenues by 20 percent in a very tight market, bringing in over 40 new clients in the first year while retaining and managing a substantial client base that included clients as far away as Korea and Denmark. Was brought in to turn this magazine around after it had been bleeding red ink for a year. In six months we had increased revenue by 60 percent and made it profitable. The group VP had never seen such an amazing turnaround and gave me full credit for it. In my first year I took this magazine, increasing revenue by 25 percent, and 20 percent each year thereafter. The magazine went from being last in ad revenue to first in a three-year period. (Abe Carter was part of XYZ Media. In 2000, the name Abe Carter was sold along with a small part of the company. They now trade under JKL Media. They are by far the market leader in high-tech and music publishing in the United States.)

ABC Press Inc., New York, NY–Advertising Director
7/1995–6/1996
Action Company: Managed the flagship account for their advertising department. This magazine had been dwindling for three years. Brought it back and exceeded the best year. Advised the society on ways to market themselves and increase membership and circulation.

Publishing Company, London, UK; Honolulu, HI
1992–1995
Managed my own international marketing and management company. Undertook a nine-month self-sufficiency eco-survey and wrote a 200-page business plan on same. Contracted to manage a growing company in Hawaii. Revamped and computerized their inventory, oversaw the acquisition of a competitor. Trained their sales managers and salespersons, then successfully set up a new branch on the mainland, again training the sales force, managing inventory, setting up warehouse, et cetera.

Other Work Experience
1973–1995
Since leaving college in 1973, I have been successful in almost all the endeavors I have taken on. I was top salesperson of the year

in 1974. I moved and joined a then major book publishing house, becoming sales manager for Northern Europe in 1978. The following year, I tried my hand at production before moving with my new husband in 1982 to help manage a cultural center in New York, where I ended up as VP/CFO. I also was the youngest sales manager, top recruiter, and top salesperson for an international financial services group.

Education: I am fluent in MS Office and ACT 4.0, use e-mail extensively, and am used to the Windows OS. I am fluent in reading both P&L and balance sheets, can do budget projections, cash flow projections, and database management. I have taken professional courses in sales management, sales, marketing, advertising (both placement and development), direct mail, and PR. BSc, State College, London, England.

Personal: I have been married nearly 20 years and have three wonderful children. I own a 21-acre spread in upstate New York, where I weekend with my family and enjoy an active lifestyle. Would consider relocating for the right offer. References available on request.

Revised Résumé

Marie Jones
1515 Elm Street   Primary Phone: 222-222-2222
New York, NY 55555   Secondary Phone: 222-222-1111
U.S.
mjones@somewhere.com

VP Sales & Marketing /   Résumé #XXXXXXXX
High-Tech Sales
OBJECTIVE   Tech-savvy executive with nearly 20 years of experience managing sales and marketing efforts for diverse companies and industries. Demonstrated ability to maximize sales volume

and transform market position from last to number two through relationship building, negotiating favorable deals, training top-performing sales teams, securing strategic alliances, developing effective marketing collateral, and closing deals with top decision makers.

Demonstrated ability to listen to prospects' needs, develop solutions to meet their goals and budgets, and build trust and respect. Held management responsibility for 120 employees, $15 million budget administration, and $12 million in annual revenue. Internationally traveled; basic French communication skills.

TARGET JOB   **Desired Job Type:** Employee
Desired Status: Full time
Site Location: On site
Career Level: Executive (SVP, EVP, VP)
Date of Availability: Less than one month

TARGET COMPANY   **Company Size:** No Preference
Category: Sales

TARGET LOCATIONS   **Relocate:** No
U.S.–New York–New York City

WORK STATUS   U.S. I am authorized to work in this country for any employer.

EXPERIENCE   4/2001–Present ABC Company New York, NY
VP Sales & Marketing
Manage sales and marketing efforts

concurrently for ABC Company—the largest pain management group in New York—and ABC Records, a start-up record label owned by ABC Company. Develop and implement business development, sales, marketing, and PR strategies to acquire new customers and retain existing accounts. Set individual and companywide sales objectives and formulate plans to expand business. Identify opportunities for strategic alliances and partnerships that further business goals. Manage corporate collateral material, including brochure and Web redesign.

Key Accomplishments:
- Recovered $1 million in accounts receivable (A/R) through implementation of software billing solution that established a net-45-day (down from 90 days) policy on A/R. The new system also reduced billing costs by 10 percent.
- Negotiated with, signed, and currently manage PR for five major performers for ABC Records. Recruited The Plantains (known in the 1970s as a top R&B band), an alliance that is expected to produce $500,000 in profits this year.
- Proposed the introduction of new services that are expected to elevate the company's image and generate $500,000 in annual revenue.
- Redesigned company Web site, creating a cutting-edge online presentation that has received commendations by the health care community and customers.
- Developed management procedures and set

up the Artist Relations Department, helping establish ABC Records as a bona fide record label.

- Created a contact database for the fledgling record label, providing a low-cost means to market to industry players and build brand awareness.

7/1996–3/2001 DEF Company New York, NY

Advertising Director/Sales Manager
Key member of management team charged with sales, account management, supervision of sales team, and coordination of advertising campaigns. Fostered long-term relationships with key accounts and helped launch new magazines and Web sites.

Key Accomplishments:

- Secured a record-setting 22 percent average annual account growth, capitalizing on relationship-building and negotiating skills to land lucrative, high-margin accounts. Achieved $1.2 million in sales in the first year alone.
- Ranked as top salesperson (out of 120) for two consecutive years based on overall increase in market share. Twice recognized for top annual Web advertising sales.
- Opened up international markets, aggressively pursuing new clients and securing contract wins in the Far East.
- Helped turn around magazine's performance, improving ranking from last position to number two in a competitive market.

- Introduced new methods for reporting, budget projections, and competitive sales analysis, forming the basis for sales training companywide.

7/1995–6/1996 ABC Press, Inc. New York, NY

Advertising Director

Oversaw advertising, trade shows, industry/networking events, and targeted print/media campaigns driving new business development and market expansion. Supervised sales and marketing team and established the Marketing Department.

Key accomplishments:
- Expanded revenue by 35 percent and achieved the largest revenue year in the company's history by persistently targeting previously untapped markets.
- Improved customer service and retention, achieving an 80 percent renewal rate and improving communication between customer service reps and clients.
- Collaborated with Webmaster to add online service offerings and improve site's design, content, and functionality.

2/1992–6/1995   Publishing Company London, England, and Honolulu, HI

CEO

Provided the strategic vision to define company goals and implement systems for sales, marketing, HR, recruitment, training, and research. Acquired competitor's business and delivered multimedia presentations to decision makers.

Key accomplishments:
- Wrote 110-page business plan for the seventh largest charitable foundation in the UK.
- Researched 300 UK-based properties and devised a scoring system to evaluate each property according to clients' specifications.
- Successfully managed a growing retail business and set up a mainland branch.

EDUCATION   1973 STATE COLLEGE London, UK

Bachelor's Degree
Major: Biochemistry; Minor: Physics

SKILLS

Skill Name	Skill Level	Last Used	Experience
B2B/B2C Sales	Expert	Currently used	20 years
Global Markets	Expert	Currently used	20 years
Sales Training	Expert	Currently used	20 years
Professional Presentations	Expert	Currently used	20 years
Account Growth	Expert	Currently used	20 years
Sales Forecasting	Expert	Currently used	20 years
e-Commerce Initiatives	Expert	Currently used	20 years
Public Relations	Expert	Currently used	20 years
Partnerships/ Alliances	Expert	Currently Used	20 years
Vendor & Customer Relationship Management	Expert	Currently Used	20 years
Closing the Deal	Expert	Currently Used	20 years
Business Plan Development	Expert	Currently Used	20 years
Team Building/ Staff Retention	Expert	Currently Used	20 years

Contract Negotiations	Expert	Currently Used	20 years

ADDITIONAL
INFORMATION Early Career: Served as sales manager for GHI Company, Birmingham, UK (10/87–1/92) and VP/CFO for Action Co., New York, NY (8/82–6/87).

Management/marketing knowledge of computer systems and their business benefits, including hardware/software (debuggers, security tools, installers, servers, routers), operating systems (Windows, UNIX/Linux), networking, and programming languages (C++, Visual Basic, Java).

Participate in ongoing training in ACT!, sales, marketing, management, and computers. Conduct numerous training seminars on topics such as sales, marketing, closing, renewing, and positioning.

Source: Monster.com

Nailing the Interview

Should you be lucky enough to land an interview, you may still have an uphill battle in your fight against age bias, often an inevitable feature of job searches for today's older workers. "We all know that bias is alive and well," says Dave Opton,

CEO and founder of ExecuNet, a professional networking organization for executives, many of whom are over fifty. "The thing that makes it tricky is that nobody with their head legally screwed on straight is going to say anything about that bias."

He's right, but it's there. Luckily, so are strategies to counteract prejudice. "What I always tell people about this age bias—which is true of any bias that runs around this planet, and there are plenty from which to choose—is that there's a spectrum," Opton says. "At one end you have these crazy liberal people where age doesn't make a difference at all, and on the other end you have a bigot whose mind will never change," and who will refuse to see older workers as anything but a lesser talent pool. "The rest of us fall somewhere in the middle."

In other words, people's opinions can be influenced. The older worker's challenge "is to anticipate age objections someone may have and develop interview tactics and strategies that address those concerns" proactively, since they'll never be overtly stated during an interview.

The key, according to experts such as author Jeri Sedlar, is to not play into the stereotypes of older workers. "There is a responsibility with the older worker," Sedlar says. It helps "to be looking good, and exhibiting plenty of energy. Your physical well-being as well as mental well-being all tie in together. If I hear someone who is fifty say, 'Oh, can you hear every ache and pain of mine?' I think, *Shut your mouth. You're only playing into age bias.*" Not that workers over fifty should suppress every physical and mental weakness or point of pain, but Sedlar's point is well taken. And in an interview, comments like that can reduce your chances of employment on the spot—due to negativity as much as age discrimination.

Moreover, Opton says, the key for fifty-plus job seekers is to **anticipate objections an interviewer may have about your age and answer them without being asked directly.** For example, if you're sixty and you think the person interviewing you may have a concern about the health or level of physical fitness of people in that age group, during the course of your interview you might drop in the fact that you ran the Chicago Marathon last year or that you bike fifteen miles three days a week. Many interviewers start off by asking the applicant to give a little background on themselves—that's the perfect opportunity to mention such information.

We'd all like to think that our lives, and particularly our careers, are based on our professional talents alone. And they usually are, for the most part. But in first-impression situations such as interviews, there's no way of getting around it: Image plays a large role in how a potential employer initially reacts and then warms to a candidate. And one of the easiest ways to offset an interviewer's potential age bias is to present a robust first impression through your appearance.

That doesn't mean going overboard—toupees and wild hair colors, for example, are usually dangerous moves, as are wearing clothes designed for someone thirty years your junior. It also doesn't mean you need to go out and spend a thousand dollars on a new suit. But it does mean dressing in more fashionable clothing—check out business attire catalogs or more subdued fashion designers, such as Ann Taylor, if you need to bring yourself up to speed on the latest office attire.

Finally, appearances aside, once you are in someone's office in the middle of an interview, the single most important thing to keep in mind is this: Listen. **Listening skills are undoubtedly the most valuable skill in corporate America today**—valuable because they are amazingly so difficult to find. In many interviews, candidates are so busy promoting themselves and their skills that they fail to listen to what an employer has to say.

That kind of behavior is painfully obvious to almost every interviewer and an almost certain way to kill your employment prospects. Stop, listen, make sure you've understood what information your interviewer wants before answering each question, and take the time to think about how best to answer. Job candidates are often so concerned with firing off an answer quickly so as not to seem slow that they get rattled and respond with a statement that fails to answer the interviewer's question.

Hopefully you've prepared for a multitude of possible questions before entering your interview. No matter how long you've been in the workplace, when you change careers you're essentially starting over, so you might as well consider yourself as new as the day you graduated from college. Thus, it pays to craft responses for questions you think an employer will ask before heading into the interview. Also, think of questions you'd like to ask—again, this is your time to figure out if this new career or job is right for you. Better to learn that now than in the first month of your newfound career or job.

Make It Happen

It won't happen overnight, but if you follow key steps you can eventually make a career change if you're committed to doing so. One of the best—and least nerve-racking—ways to find out if a new career is right for you is to conduct professional test runs. If you want to leave your job as an accountant and become an events planner, for example, volunteer for a local fes-

tival or philanthropic group, since such groups are always looking for volunteers to help coordinate and carry out events.
Doing so will give you a good idea of what is involved in such a
job, the hours you can expect to work, the level of stress such a
job brings with it, and—ultimately—whether or not it's something you enjoy doing. If you do like it, that's also a great way
to meet people already working within the field who can connect you with other industry contacts or inform you of any job
openings.

Proving Your Worth

It's hard enough to get your foot in the door early in your career.
But when you're over fifty, the chances of finding an employer
eager to take a chance on someone starting a career from
scratch can be slim to none. So you need a strong strategy.

For starters, seek out companies that are open and eager to
hiring older workers. You'll have a much easier time convincing
them of your skills and commitment to their workplace. Check
out the AARP list of best companies for workers over fifty in
appendix A.

PART II

Jobs for the Older Worker

Chapter 4

Why Part-Time Work Pays

Part-time work is playing a large role in the phenomenon of older Americans returning to work or looking to change their current work situations, and for good reason. While a lot of older workers are hesitant about the notion of retiring permanently, many are ready to relax their grip on full-time employment as well as ease the burden of stress-inducing responsibilities. Working part time offers them the financial and professional flexibility they're craving.

The need for such work experiences has probably increased in recent years as more older workers head into retirement, but also as a result of corporations slashing headcounts—and not just because those let go couldn't find full-time work again, although it is a temporary solution for those trying to bridge the gap from one job to the next. Events such as 9/11 and corporate scandals have profoundly shifted Americans' attitudes toward the importance of daily work and careers, and readjusted their views on work–life balances. Time spent with family, friends, and activities outside work has suddenly taken on a new significance.

Others who've been laid off have decided they've had enough of the corporate downsizing that has ravaged company staffs and left employees demoralized. Why put up with the heartache of being let go, and hustle through another stressful job search, only to risk being let go once more somewhere down the line? Part-time workers can certainly suffer the cuts of the corporate ax, but it's also work that's more easily picked up again. Emotional investment is sometimes more limited than in a full-time career, making for a less painful departure if you are asked to leave.

When Part-Time Work Makes Sense

If all this seems like a lot of introspection and analysis all in the name of part-time employment—well, perhaps. But certain individuals are living proof that working part time can be just as enriching as a full-time career. And part-time jobs don't have to be of the typical grocery-store bag-boy variety. For example, one fifty-plus worker in Tucson, Arizona, has become a master at turning his hobbies into part-time work. At an area Elderhostel, he began offering workshops in areas of expertise he's picked up throughout his life, such as big-band music, bread making, and digital photography. As each class became popular, he'd consider what he could teach next as a way to keep himself enthused about his work. And he found a willing audience.

Working part time during retirement is often ideal for all involved. It keeps older workers engaged in the workplace, generally with easy hours and little stress; gives them extra income to ease living expenses; and provides a much-needed talent pool for companies. It's also one of the easiest ways to break into working after you've left a long career—and part-time work rarely burdens workers with the heavy responsibilities that come with full-time employment for mid- to upper-level managers.

If you're looking for managerial or office work on a part-time basis, **plenty of temporary agencies are out there with offices nationwide looking to hire older workers specifically for their skills, reliability, and work ethic.** But if you want to make yourself really valuable at a staffing firm, make sure you've mastered basic word processing software programs, common e-mail systems, and even applications such as Microsoft Excel. Doing so will put you at the head of the pack when it comes to doling out assignments and future long-term work.

There's also a good chance you'll stand out against younger employees if you exhibit the great work ethic, conscientious attitude, and attention to detail that many staffing agencies have come to equate with their older temporary talent pool. Michael Dowhan, a former executive who's now a part-time bookseller at Barnes & Noble, says managers at the store admire his consistency, work ethic, and professional attitude. "I get my hair cut and I wear a white shirt, I don't spend time in the bathroom, and I'm not outside sneaking a smoke," Dowhan jokes, comparing himself with younger workers whose attire or appearance might be sloppier. But his real value to store managers, he says, is that he's not going anywhere. "Once the young ones graduate from college, they're gone." And his commitment to the workplace is often higher than is seen among younger workers, who are often simply earning pay while they work toward something else. "One co-worker said, 'You work twice as hard as the people half your age,'" Dowhan notes.

Plenty of companies are realizing the same thing: that older, part-time workers can fill critical labor gaps better than a younger workforce could. The difference is that the high rates of turnover seen when part-time jobs are filled by teens and college students just don't happen when those same jobs are filled by people in their retirement years.

This is not to mention the benefits to the workers themselves. Part-time work can be a way to participate in more than one industry, exploring multiple interests without committing to one company.

Arthur Levine, a former banking executive, knows that well. In the mid-1990s, he was downsized at age forty-five and left to figure out a new professional move in the prime of his career. He has realized now that he's in his fifties that work can consist of a smattering of part-time jobs. He's been a part-time newspaper columnist, candy machine vendor (his license plate reads MR. CANDY), factory worker, and, most recently, cashier at a Wal-Mart in York, Pennsylvania. "In order to survive I did part-time jobs," says Levine, whose wife works in the accounts payable office of a local hospital. But it dawned on him in the course of taking on those jobs that juggling several at once infuses his work experience with a freshness that one steady, full-time job does not. Like Dowhan, he has no plans to quit. Levine sees retirement not as a permanent vacation, but as a time to seek out work that's socially gratifying and provides a daily sense of purpose.

Indeed, the American Association of Retired Persons has long advocated part-time work for older workers. Ever since the Senior Community Service Employment Program (SCSEP) was formed in the 1960s to help Americans living at or below the poverty line find part-time work experiences to develop skills

and gain employment, AARP has done much to further opportunities for mature workers, especially in the form of part-time
work. You can find your state SCSEP offices by going to the
AARP Web site at http://www.aarp.org/scsep-locate/.

More recently, the organization has developed special programs such as the National Hiring Partnership it formed with
Home Depot in February 2004. This partnership is an initiative
to hire "qualified, skilled, mature workers"—individuals fifty-
five and older—into Home Depot's hundreds of stores nationwide. Workers are sought for positions that range from part-time
sales associates to full-time store managers. Benefits are available for part-timers as well as those who work a full week.

Not all part-time work, however, is hourly employment.
Plenty of mid- to upper-level managers are finding part-time
opportunities through staffing agencies and industry groups
looking to tap into the wisdom of former professionals who
have since retired.

"You hear about folks getting to retirement at sixty-five and
then dropping dead three months later," says Glenn McAvoy,
fifty-two, and a former CFO for the University Physicians, a
practice within the University of Maryland School of Medicine,
until June 2000. So rather than plan on quitting cold turkey at
sixty-five, he's been tiptoeing out of a full-time career for several
years through part-time assignments. "It's been my aim for the
past fifteen years to find work for three or four days a week,"
McAvoy says. In 2001, he found part-time work through staffing
firm Spherion at national learning center Sylvan, working out of
its corporate office three days a week to manage the company's
budget and reporting mechanisms while Sylvan executives
searched for a new CFO.

It doesn't hurt that McAvoy is able to maintain a decent income as he works on a part-time basis. A portfolio that lacked diversity was nevertheless doing well up to 2000, when technology stock prices dropped—and with them the value of McAvoy's portfolio, by more than 40 percent. The only saving grace was that he'd sold off half of one explosively growing stock before the firm was investigated by the Securities and Exchange Commission (SEC) and found to be guilty of accounting fraud.

The drop in his nest egg propelled McAvoy back to work, but the appeal of part-time employment is what has kept him there. He says he is convinced that "the secret to longevity is keeping your mind engaged." His next career interest is in teaching, which he hopes to do on a high school level for several years—a job that is certainly full time, but also features frequent time off. "Maybe by the time I'm seventy-five or eighty, I'll have had enough," he says, then adds that then he may join the Peace Corps. The only barrier he foresees is the ability to consistently find gratifying part-time work. "I don't see myself working in a Blockbuster," he says. "It's more about where can you add value and proficiency" on an executive, strategic level.

Is Part-Time Work for You?

If you're not sure how to answer that question, it may be that part-time work isn't the appropriate work choice for you right now. But it could also mean that you haven't properly explored all the options part-time work can offer to individuals, including the freedom to be employed but still have time for hobbies, family, community activities, or another line of work. The best way to figure out what type of part-time employment might be ideal for you is to consider your lifestyle, your finances, and any other family or community obligations that would affect the hours and type of work you might do. Consider the following:

- How many hours a week are you willing to commit to working?
- A better question might be: How many hours do you need to work at a minimum to meet your living expenses? Then look for jobs that meet those hourly needs.
- Do you want a part-time job that will keep you moving on your feet in a retail setting, or would you prefer light office work for a few hours a day? Don't forget about jobs that may provide unique work environments outdoors, for example.
- Expand your vision of what constitutes part-time work. Web sites such as Craigslist (see Where to Find It, below) are great places to peruse because they list unusual jobs most people would never think of on their own but would be delighted to participate in. For example, the San Francisco page of Craigslist has included postings for a part-time food taster (which pays forty dollars for one hour of work) and a job as a bilingual study interviewer (which pays as much as sixteen hundred dollars a month for less than twenty-five hours of work a week).
- Is part-time work enough professional stimulation and challenge for you, or do you still need a little more of the pressure-cooker environment that a full-time job can offer?
- Will part-time work offer you opportunities that you might not have with full-time employment, such as more

time to spend with your family or pursuing interests that a fifty-hour-a-week job didn't permit?

Part-Time Work: Where to Find It

Luckily, the search for part-time work is typically easier than the hunt for full-time employment in the twilight of a career. But it still helps to keep a few tips in mind while looking:

◆ **Go Online.** Plenty of listings for part-time employment can easily be found on the Internet. The Web site www.snagajob.com lists dozens of part-time jobs, from office work to retail employment, searchable by zip code. One of the best job-search engines for part-time work is Craigslist at www.craigslist.com. The brilliance of this Web site is that it has mastered the art of functioning as an electronic community bulletin board. It consists of series of postings about everything from housing to pet supplies to personal ads for forty-eight different cities across the country and nine destinations around the world. Fortunately, employment listings are plentiful and ever changing.

◆ **Consider the Season.** Seasonal work—extra department-store help during the holidays, for example—frequently offers a great opportunity for part-time employment, as well as a way to transition into full-time work if you need more. Just about any major retailer will be looking for seasonal workers come Thanksgiving and Christmas. Those holiday employees who are reliable and productive are often asked to stay on as permanent part-timers once the holiday rush has passed.

◆ **Temporary Agencies.** As with full-time employment searches, staffing agencies are a rich source of opportunities for people looking to work just a few hours a day or a few days a week. Check agencies in your area for those that may be more inclined to find jobs for older workers. Jobs can range from manual labor to work in executive offices.

◆ **Retiree Organizations.** Groups such as AARP are focused on providing work opportunities for people over fifty. AARP's Senior Community Service Employment Program, for example, offers work-training programs for lower-income seniors looking to get back to work.

◆ **Call the Classic Outlets.** Companies like Home Depot and Wal-Mart have a reputation for seeking out older workers, and they are a good place to start your search. Don't think that because you apply for a job at Home Depot, you're limited to checkout duty. There are a variety of part-time jobs. Under the company's partner-ship with AARP, mature workers are encouraged to apply for part-time work in almost every department.

◆ **Wander Through Your Community.** Often the best part-time jobs are found simply by asking owners of small shops or businesses in your area if they need additional help. Make a point of making the rounds to some of the places you think you'd like to work. **Small businesses are often more amenable to part-time hours** and provide an environment where you can have more of a presence than you might as a shelf stocker in the cavernous warehouses of giant box retailers.

◆ **Scan the Paper.** It's probably the oldest method of looking for a job, but it remains one of the best. Look through print editions of weekly circulars. Classified ads are often a big part of such papers' revenue, so these publications are packed with job openings, par-ticularly for part-time positions.

Chapter 5

The Attraction of Former Employees

For thirty-five years, Mike Burns developed what any talented organic chemist at Procter & Gamble would: household products. Namely laundry, fabric, and other home care items in the consumer goods product category that he and his colleagues meticulously tweaked over the years, with Burns specializing in bleach technology. That's a lot of time spent mastering the nuances of Tide, Downy, and Mr. Clean. And P&G knows it. Which is why it developed YourEncore, an independent, for-profit organization that the Cincinnati company and its partner, Eli Lilly, have partly subsidized to tap the expertise of an earlier generation of scientists.

YourEncore brings back former employees like Burns to work part time on various projects, and recruits other chemists, engineers, and scientists from a variety of companies who have retired but miss the work they dedicated so many years to. Since the program's launch in September 2003, 350 scientists and engineers from the aerospace, communications, chemical, consumer products, health care, and pharmaceutical industries have been brought out of retirement to offer younger colleagues help and expertise on various projects.

Brad Lawson, YourEncore's CEO, likes to mention the group's stats: over a hundred PhDs, more than seventy-five hundred years of combined experience, and talented, highly skilled, high-level research and development experts in their fields plucked from careers at seventy-five different companies. And that's all under the efforts of a passive recruitment program where most of the participants are referred by word of mouth.

What appeals to these former members of the science world—where a rich sense of community is often pervasive—is returning to a robust network of peers that they can tap into but on a limited, less stressful basis. "The feeling of belonging is important versus having belongings," Lawson says, suggesting that **remaining involved, at least in part, with their former profession is an important element in retirees' happiness.**

For Burns, being involved in YourEncore has meant a much more enriching professional life as he moves into his senior years. "My intent in retirement was to stay active, and I actually did some consulting," Burns says. "But I had planned to do that 25 percent of the time and it was actually more like 10 or 15 percent," despite an arrangement to consult on occasion for his former employer, P&G.

After a year, Burns, aware that consulting gigs were trickling in—not pouring in, as he had hoped—considered his next move: spending hundreds, if not thousands, of dollars to market his practice online. That seemed like a logical strategy, but also a tactic that involved a substantial amount of money without a guaranteed return on investment. Then Lawson called, and Burns soon became a part of the organization. "It was a fairly large commitment, because it would be working half time, and that looks like a lot when you're retired," Burns says. But "after some pretty heavy consultation with my wife, we agreed that I would go back to work half time," which averages out to about thirty hours a week.

Since then, Burns has been a relationship manager for YourEncore, promoting and managing the company's projects with clients. And while the half-time work arrangement has expanded, there have been some rewarding changes. Since YourEncore consists of only a few hundred people, the level of productivity—given the absence of bureaucracy and the normal time lag with which a behemoth like P&G operates—has meant that "you can do in three-quarters time what it took you to do in twice that time at a large company." That kind of pace has reinvigorated Burns's interest in his work at an age when he thought his career might be winding down, not gearing up.

Pay for YourEncore employees is calculated based upon what they made before they retired then adjusted for inflation, with bonuses added where needed. But benefits aren't included in the relationship, which is more like a consultative one.

The rehiring of former employees is an increasingly common practice, and one open to many retirees looking to keep a hand in the work that stimulated them in their careers. For companies such as Procter & Gamble and Eli Lilly, it helps fill gaps in departments short on staffing resources and provides mentors to a younger generation that may not know older but still important techniques for product development. Burns, for instance, "got a phone call recently where someone at P&G was trying to remember one particular aspect of Tide with Bleach. . . . I've come back to P&G and given presentations on how to review from a historical perspective certain [product] technologies."

Retirees who hold expertise that younger workers simply don't have are an invaluable tool for companies, which can quickly pull information from older workers rather than retrain an entire new generation. "In a consumer product, there are a tremendous number of facets," Burns says, "not only the technology but the product's formulation, regulatory concerns, packaging" and myriad other elements. Project teams can involve as many as sixty people—from the scientist perfecting bleach technology to the graphic designer polishing the package's label. It's cumbersome to insert additional training into such teams when previous workers can be so easily brought back for quicker, less expensive training sessions on topics they spent careers mastering.

What's always at risk with these programs is a generation gap. Will younger workers respect their older mentors and appreciate the skills they can pass on, or will they see them, particularly in fields as progressive as science and technology, as dinosaurs who must grudgingly be listened to? There is, on occasion, resistance to the opinions and ideas of YourEncore participants among younger workers at P&G and Eli Lilly, but those instances have so far been few and far between, says Burns. For the most part, younger workers "treat them with respect and appreciate the experience they bring." And older workers can facilitate the process by showing respect for what younger workers have to teach, being careful about not taking an authoritative tone, and making sure they're up to speed on the latest news and technology in their field.

Who Wants Me Back?

Ed Carrington retired in 1997 from his position as vice president of human resources for Hercules, a chemical manufacturer in Wilmington, Delaware, and returned three years later as a consultant to help stabilize the company. "I went out early" at fifty-five, Carrington says, and moved to Sanibel Island in Florida, an exclusive community where executives from corporations such as General Motors and IBM might go to retire, and where he imagined his dream career would be launched. He invested in property and began a business in which he bought, remodeled, and sold homes.

Carrington had become enamored of the place on a previous vacation. "In Florida, you get the sand between your toes. It seemed idyllic." Then local politics surfaced. Carrington admits that he entrenched himself in the political battles that eventually drove him away. Sanibel Island Chamber of Commerce directors, he says, were obligated to protect commerce and business owners who lived on the island. In Carrington's mind, that meant keeping external competition out. So when the chamber started soliciting bids for business from companies not based on the island, Carrington and another colleague filed a lawsuit against the chamber. "A judge agreed that they violated their charter and ordered a new election for chamber directors"—a result, unfortunately, that didn't leave Carrington too popular with the locals. Eventually some residents even avoided speaking to Carrington.

Nearly fed up with his situation by 2000, Carrington was considering options away from Sanibel when "I got a call from Hercules and they asked me if I'd come back." Acquisitions during the dot-com boom that Hercules had paid for in cash had left the company with a massive debt that it simply couldn't manage. "They were on the brink of disaster and wanted me to come back and help rebuild."

An interim assignment eventually turned into full-time work again. "It turned out to be a great decision. It was like taking a three-year sabbatical as a business owner, and I came back with a keen sense on how to make payrolls more economical," Carrington says, thanks to managing a lower operating budget within his own business. "I have the same title as before, but now I'm really challenged and excited. I do a lot more global stuff. I'm happy doing this for five years or more."

Recalling the Troops

Companies such as Prudential, Chevron, and Deloitte led the way in rehiring retirees in the late 1990s, crafting programs that used older workers and former employees as consultants and part-time contractors. Stories in business magazines reported how corporate recruiters couldn't do enough to maintain contact with and attract former employees back into the ranks amid the massive talent crunch of the dot-com boom.

Events of that time, including paranoia about Y2K, for instance, gave ample opportunity to people like COBOL programmers, many of whom were in their fifties, to come back to corporate offices and rework computer systems that companies feared were doomed to dysfunction come January 1, 2000. Mature workers back in the mix were reported to pull in a hundred dollars an hour, says Bill Payson, who helped found Legacy Reserves, an online staffing firm for information technology professionals whose members are over the age of thirty-five, but often much older. Their actual hourly pay was somewhere much lower than that, Payson adds, but the fact that older IT professionals felt needed sparked people looking to reenter the market to return in droves.

As the number of Web-based companies was exploding and public offerings became the corporate norm, experts talked of the need for management strategies that could deal with "inter-generational" conflict resolution. Schedules would have to be modified. Younger workers would need to be open to absorbing the wisdom and skill sets that older mentors could pass down to them. Suddenly age discrimination had taken a turn in older workers' favor.

Then just as quickly as the bubble had expanded, it collapsed. The dot-com boom went bust, and downsizing became the order of the day. First to be cut were thousands of midlevel managers, many of whom were over fifty or nearing retirement.

Suddenly ageism was again a creeping concern for those out of work looking to reenter the marketplace. Of course, that doesn't stop older workers from wanting to return and reinvigo-rate their minds working at former employers, even if getting there may be a little more difficult today than it was five years ago. "There's lots of stuff written about preparing yourself for retirement, but it's too much about preparing financially and not intellectually," says Carrington. **Americans don't realize what a jolt suddenly leaving their jobs can be.** In fact, Carring-ton notes, it can propel them right back to their former offices.

In recent years, progressive, proactive companies have been looking once more at ways to reengage older workers. Yet for all the talk of corporate America waking to the new age of mature workers, the reality is that the awakening is a slow one at best. With industries focused tightly on how to raise profit margins in a tougher and tougher market, the idea of how older workers can play a larger role in the company's daily operations is dropping to the bottom of corporate America's agenda—even though placing it higher on the list of priorities could put more able-bodied individuals inside a company and improve its productivity.

Some industries and companies do show promise in courting staffers over fifty, of course. Health care organizations, such as local hospitals and regional medical centers, are increasingly providing work programs for older employees. Employment crises within the medical industry have, in part, helped push the movement. Nursing shortages reached epic proportions years ago and continue to burden the industry today, spurring some medical centers to offer perks such as scholarships for nurses who may still need schooling in an effort to recruit new staff.

In the 2004 AARP awards citing the thirty-five best employers for older workers, twelve of the award recipients were hospitals, four were in financial services, and three were providers of insurance. Technology companies, particularly in Silicon Valley, have also been noted for their earnest attempt to reach out to older workers.

Plenty of individuals over fifty are ready to walk away from the daily grind of high-level positions. But they're not ready to unplug from that world to spend their days weeding their vegetable gardens or mastering a vicious backhand. Rather, they'd like to develop new interests and hobbies but also maintain a certain level of involvement in their previous industry.

So just how many companies are really embracing this phenomenon? Sadly, not the majority. In a recent survey by the Society for Human Resource Management, 62 percent of HR professionals surveyed said that the increasing number of older workers is having little or no impact on recruitment, retention, and management practices.

"I came out of more than twenty years in Fortune 500 companies, and I think companies are pretty shortsighted in general," says Martin Rome, vice president of strategic communications for Experience Works Inc., an online employment site for older workers. "Any public company looks quarter to quarter, and they don't look far down the road." But the dearth of workers that will settle in when baby boomers leave the workplace is real—and looming, he says. Yet for now, at least, it seems most companies are waiting to cross that bridge when they come to it.

"It's clear that in 2007 it's going to be really bad. And by 2010 there won't be enough labor to meet the needs of business in this country. No amount of immigration will make that work. Companies will have to tap into older workers," Rome continues, suggesting that organizations will have to give the same attention to an aging workforce that they did to diversity issues fifteen years ago. Those firms already doing so will be that much farther ahead of the game when hauling back seniors becomes critical.

The Principal Financial Group, based in Des Moines, Iowa, began what it calls its Happy Returns program slightly ahead of the curve in 1996 to tap the talents and knowledge of former employees. The program, which has been honored three years in a row by AARP on its list of Best Employers for Workers Over 50, works by rehiring retired employees through the temporary agency Manpower, which pulls them into the workplace without affecting their retirement benefits. Principal also uses the program to entice workers who are nearing retirement to remain with the company longer, albeit as Manpower staffers. In that scenario, employees can quit and be rehired as early as the next week by Manpower to finish projects.

The program is small in the number of employees who have participated during its eight-year run—only fifty to date—and attracts staff largely through word of mouth or department referral, but it is steadily expanding. Employees can work part time or full time, but the value of doing so through Happy

Returns is that this circumvents pension plan restrictions that deny employees retirement payments while they continue to work at the same employer. There's a huge benefit to Principal as well. "These employees obviously care about the company and enjoy working for Principal and add value that way," says Rhonda Clark-Leyda, senior media relations consultant with Principal. "They also have experience with the areas they're working in and with the company's business. When you compare a retiree with a temporary worker who doesn't have the same experience, it's an obvious benefit to the company."

For the most part, work through Happy Returns is conducted in low-stress, high-activity areas such as the mail department where employees sort incoming and outgoing correspondence, averaging, in any given department, about three days of work a week. Others work in accounting—as receptionists, for example—or within other areas where their services may be needed. "One of the main things we see is that employees don't choose to be in the thick of projects doing high-stress work," says Gini Wolf, a manager at Manpower who works on site at Principal coordinating hiring for the Happy Returns program. "One of the goals of Happy Returns employees is that they want to come in and do something that's not stressful and more routine in nature, and they don't want to take work home with them at night." But they do want to continue to earn money, be engaged in some capacity in the workplace, remain involved with a firm that they respect, and feel that they're a vital part of the company's daily operations and productivity.

Of Principal's fifteen thousand employees, 17 percent are fifty or older. Wolf believes this will encourage the company to maintain or even expand its Happy Returns program in the years ahead. "As we go into the next ten years, I would guess that

Principal would be promoting this program in an aggressive way," she says. "We know what's happening to the labor force in the next ten years. We have a huge population leaving the workplace with seventy-six million boomers ready to retire in 2011. And as the Social Security age keeps increasing, in the years we can retire we will see people staying in the workforce longer and longer."

And like other firms facing boomer retirement, Principal will need the long-term loyalty of these employees to remain success-ful and productive in its market. "It is flexibility that is so important at this time," Wolf adds, "and I think that their loy-alty to the company is enhanced" through Happy Returns. "They're already loyal employees and have been for many years. This is just one more continuation of that goodwill and company benefits."

Mary Lu Baumbach would probably agree. A thirteen-year employee with Principal, she joined the Happy Returns pro-gram in April 2004 and now works as a receptionist at the Prin-cipal Employee Financial Center. For Baumbach, the program is ideal. As a "housemaker," as she puts it, who wasn't a part of the labor market for twenty-five years while she raised her nine children, Baumbach hadn't developed an overwhelming amount of business skills. A 1985 divorce left her facing the stark reality that she needed to support herself financially. In 1990, she found work at Principal and proceeded to jump from depart-ment to department enjoying the variety of tasks and co-workers she encountered within each. "I thought as long as I'm going to be here, I wanted to get as much exposure to the company as I could," Baumbach says. So she moved through departments including group records, human resources, information tech-nology, the corporate library, and the company's own Principal

Bank, filing corporate documents, assembling crucial paper-work, filling in as an administrative assistant, and disseminating new-account information along the way.

Then in March 2003, Baumbach decided it was time to call it quits. She was sixty-five and thought, "I'll read and have more time for gardening." But it didn't take her long to realize that "there's more to life than gardening." That led to a job as a hostess at the Ingersoll Dinner Theater in Des Moines where she lives. When she heard about the Happy Returns program, though, she admitted to herself that her finances could use a further boost. Since April 2004, she's worked on a part-time basis—perhaps three hours one day and four the next, or all day for a week then off for two. The sporadic hours are part of the appeal, Baumbach says, offering her the periodic motivation in the office she enjoys but still giving her plenty of time to manage a retirement lifestyle that includes volunteering, dinner theaters, her children—and some occasional gardening. She also likes the fact that returning through Manpower allows her to keep collecting her Principal pension.

"I'm a high-energy person and I don't really care to sit still too long," Baumbach says, adding that working into retirement is crucial for older Americans to maintain their physical and emotional health. "If you're going to sit in a rocking chair on your porch, you're going to rock yourself to an early grave."

There may be truth to Baumbach's rocking-chair theory. There's plenty of evidence to suggest that **idleness can lead to boredom, depression, and even a declining interest in carrying on.**

Fortunately, Principal isn't alone in establishing programs allowing retirees to come back to work. An increasing number of companies—albeit a slow-moving minority of them—are

looking at ways to target former employees and other potential
older workers. The reason: Corporate HR professionals know
that recently retired individuals already equipped with the necessary skills for a given position are far more valuable to a company than new hires who have to be trained from scratch, which
can run hundreds, even thousands of dollars per employee.

How can you exploit this phenomenon?

- ◆ If you've recently left the workplace or have even been
  absent for a while and want to return to work, your best
  shot may be through a past employer, even if the company doesn't have a formalized program to recruit back
  former staff members.
- ◆ It's a good idea to gather contact information on key
  company staffers, such as departmental colleagues and
  HR leaders, when you retire and keep in touch with
  them on a regular basis. That makes coming back that
  much easier if you do decide to return, and gives you a
  solid network of folks with whom you can feel out areas
  where there may be staffing gaps, then discuss how you
  could be of benefit on a part-time or contractual, freelance basis.
- ◆ Be patient and considerate; it may take time to get a
  response, even from people you formerly worked with.
- ◆ As with any reentry for older workers, stress the specific
  talents that you can bring to the company as well as any
  additional skills you've picked up since your departure.

Pension Tricks of the Trade

There have been plenty of discussions in the past few years about the penalties people may suffer when they return to work for a former employer after retiring. There are sometimes penalties for withdrawing from a pension plan. But for the most part, the short answer is this: Penalties are specific to your company. Certainly, the IRS has no qualms about former staffers returning to their last employer for part-time or full-time work. Some pension plans are set up, however, such that working more than a certain number of hours per week can jeopardize your ability to make withdrawals. If you think this is a potential roadblock, check with your employer first. Many companies are revisiting and redrafting their pension policies expressly with the purpose of allowing former employees to return to the workplace.

Going Back to a New Future

Returning to a former employer doesn't have to mean going back and sitting at your same desk surrounded by the people you said good-bye to just six months ago. (Not that there's anything wrong with that!) If you're itching to return to your field, but in a new environment, now's the time to look at a new company within your area of expertise.

That strategy has allowed people like Stephen Fritz, the former academic mentioned in chapter 1, to float among colleges and universities—always remaining within education, but applying his administrative skills on various campuses around the country. "Doing so allows me an opportunity to draw upon all of my experience in higher education and academic administration and concentrate it in a way that persons who come into so-called permanent positions don't have," Fritz says.

Back in the Mix

Want to return to your old employer—or at least your old field—after a few years out of the loop? It's entirely possible. But it may take a little ingenuity, legwork, and patience to get there:

◆ **Reconnect with Colleagues. The best place to start a new job search may be at the last place you left.** Call old colleagues, supervisors, and industry contacts (if you're a smart networker, you haven't lost touch with them) and let anyone and everyone know that you are interested in going back to work.

◆ **Get a Handle on the Market.** Depending on when you left the workforce, a lot could have happened in your field and particularly the last company you worked for—additional competition, new products, technology developments, corporate redirections, and other changes. Make sure you research your company and industry (old colleagues are a good start) by reading the business press, keeping up with trade magazines, and conducting research online, so you have a handle on what you're getting back into and where you may picture yourself working. This might be a good time to query former workers about any changes in culture, structure, or management styles at the organization in which you used to work.

◆ **Refresh Your Skills.** If you have an obscure skill still in demand that you know younger workers won't possess, you can always tout it when trying to reenter your profession of choice. But there's also a chance that your previous forte is no longer bankable. If you're in the information technology field, for example, there have undoubtedly been new computer developments that require updated skills. It will be easier to prove your worth if you acquired these new talents while you were away from the firm.

◆ **Update Your Résumé.** Unless you're absolutely sure retirement is your calling beyond the age of fifty, you should always keep an updated résumé, something that highlights the most recent use of your skills—even if it's managing projects for community organizations or volunteer groups. If you want to get back into the workplace, you'll need proof that you're still up to the task. Review résumé-writing skills in chapter 3 if you need help reworking your current résumé.

Chapter 6

Fulfilling Your Entrepreneurial Dreams

Marianne D'Eugenio had had enough. After twenty-five years in accounting at St. Mary's Hospital, in Waterbury, Connecticut, nothing about work inspired her. It hadn't always been that way. In her successful career there, she'd risen from an accounting clerk to an internal auditor and had been recognized for her talents along the way. But then something happened. "I don't know if it's because I turned fifty and things weren't fun anymore, but it was really difficult to get up and go to work every day," D'Eugenio says. That was in 1997, when Clinton was president, "health care was in flux, and everyone was so edgy," she recalls. "I said, 'Forget it, I don't want to be director of anything anymore.' I left that job and decided I would do something menial, that I wasn't going to retire as a stressed-out person."

Then she tripped—literally—and was laid up off her feet for six weeks with a broken ankle. Boredom set in, D'Eugenio says, and she began considering her options. St. Mary's started to offer her consulting jobs, which she loved, since she was stimulated by the work but removed from the stress of working there full time. But eventually even consulting became uninspiring. "I started thinking that part of the reason why I left the hospital was that I was no longer able to be creative," she says. "Everything had been set in its place because I had been there so long."

That's when D'Eugenio discovered free courses at her area's Small Business Administration (SBA) offices. "I got a list of classes, and one was how to write a business plan." She attended her first class in April 2002, nearly broke without an income, and slowly started building her plan to open a quilting shop—which had been her hobby for thirty-five years—a storefront business that didn't exist, as far as she could tell, anywhere between North Haven and Cheshire, Connecticut, the two towns that sandwiched hers. Her only real asset was her home, which was nearly paid for. She mortgaged it, and, with some additional financial help from friends and family, plunked down the monthly rent of $750 for a twelve-hundred-square-foot former beauty shop in the middle of Waterbury. Then, slowly, bit by bit, reality hit. She would need laborers—and fast—to strip down the shop's walls and floors and refurbish them. Friends and family helped revitalize the store, and a cousin donated shelves. But there were other major concerns: She had no merchandise ("I had forgotten about that," she says). No staff. No marketing plan. And, most important, no customers. With an approaching opening of October 2002, D'Eugenio began calling other quilting shops around the Northeast that September, asking where they got their supplies and fabric bolts. "It never dawned on me that [supplies] would take six months to come in." She only had thirty days.

So she got creative. With a hundred thousand dollars from her home's mortgage, she bought two hundred bolts of fabric from an area retailer. "I put them on the shelves and this place was still totally bare," she says, laughing. She called friends to bring over quilts and flowers to fill the void until she could afford more bolts of fabric. "We filled the shelves with anything we could."

It didn't take long. Two years later, her stock of bolts hovers around two thousand, and her shelves are packed with quilting tools and other amenities to make her store a one-stop shop for quilting enthusiasts. In addition, her staff has ballooned from a few family and friends to twenty-five teachers who offer classes five days a week to the community. "Now I have no room in this place," D'Eugenio says. "If you asked me two and a half years ago, I couldn't wait to turn sixty-two so I could start collecting Social Security. I was going to do nothing. Now I don't think about it. I love what I do, and I have no regrets about leaving the health care industry."

D'Eugenio's story may sound familiar. Small businesses continue to be an explosive part of the economy. Perhaps residual inspiration from the dot-com boom still lurks in the minds of budding entrepreneurs—or flourishes there despite its collapse. Regardless, there seem to be thousands of tales like D'Eugenio's every day—stories of Americans who are fed up with corporate politics, are victims of staff cuts, or are inspired by their passions, and who decide to launch a business. The reality, however, isn't so generous. Nine out of ten independent businesses fail within the first five years, says George Knauf, a business start-up consultant with GC Alliance. Why? "Most people didn't have any idea what they were doing," says Knauf, who specializes in helping individuals launch franchises. "You have to have a lot of faith to go forward."

Plenty of Americans have found that faith—some 40 percent of whom are older than fifty, according to an AARP study. In fact, **baby boomers are leading the way in new-business ventures,** according to experts.

Follow Your Dream

It's a common dream to open your own business, and, for many Americans, retirement or the late-career years represent a time when they see themselves as older, more mature, and educated by corporate experience to the point that they can invest part of their nest egg in their own venture. A large portion of business owners spend time considering the perfect company to start, but plenty of others stumble into an opportunity that they never would have otherwise considered.

That was the case with Donald Devine, sixty-two, owner of the Lighthouse Depot, a retail store and catalog business that he founded in Maine after redecorating a room in his house with a lighthouse theme and realizing he was intrigued by the structures. He'd spent thirty years at Norton Abrasives, the manufacturer of sandpaper and other finishing and polishing materials, climbing through twenty-two positions on the corporate ladder until he ended his career there as an international division president with a salary that had grown fiftyfold since he'd joined the firm just out of college as a staff assistant.

But he felt less inspired and challenged after the company was purchased by French behemoth Saint-Gobain. So he left at fifty-three with more than enough money to live out his life. And, for all he knew, that might just happen.

His life changed when he added a room to his house in Maine. Devine told his wife he would complete the room's design with a nautical theme. That's when he read about the world's largest lighthouse gift store in Maine. "I hightailed it up there and spent a thousand dollars and finished off the room" with a bounty of lighthouses—and picked up a small-business idea in the process.

As Devine looked into lighthouses further, he realized their popularity among consumers and started to build a rapport with the owners of the lighthouse store he'd recently visited. He eventually negotiated with them to start a catalog business out of their store and ultimately launched an initial mailing of four hundred thousand catalogs. The business has since grown to distribute more than six million catalogs a month and seen sales balloon to more than ten million in 2003. "In the catalog industry, if you sell one dollar per catalog that's good," says Devine. "We did over two dollars a book" on the first mailing. "It was a home run."

Is Owning a Business Right for Me?

Forget, for the moment, what type of business you want to build. The real question is: Do you even want to start one? For mid- or upper-level managers in corporate America, launching a business may seem a logical step—a place where they can transfer the skills they learned during their career in a major company and have a sense of ownership in doing so. But for folks with less managerial experience, is founding a business the right move?

Budding entrepreneurs should know what they're getting into, particularly former high-level managers. "Executives spend twenty or thirty years building their ego and titles," Knauf says. "They ride around on a corporate jet. Now someone says, 'Here are the keys to the store. Go open it every morning at 6 AM. It's culture shock, but if you want to build a business empire, this is step one."

Once he learned of the daily slog through menial chores that opening a business posed, for instance, one former Citicorp executive decided to take a lower-paying corporate position rather than open his own business, according to Knauf. Smart move. Even franchises—where much of the upfront legwork, like marketing plans, comes prepackaged—demand hard labor from business owners.

Still, plenty of people, from all levels of corporate America, have successfully opened businesses. And even more are likely to do so. An August 2004 report from outplacement firm Challenger, Gray & Christmas, Inc. noted that the number of senior-level executives in the United States starting their own business had doubled in the first two quarters of that year. New companies started by managers and executives out of work, who earned six-figure-plus salaries in their previous jobs, increased 96 percent from 2003 to 2004. Starting new businesses may stem from desperation and disgust with opportunities within corporate America as much as from an eagerness for or confidence in small-business success, the report concluded. Regardless, statistics show that more and more Americans fifty and older are venturing out in their own companies, many successfully.

Of course, there's a secret to success: Those who become accomplished entrepreneurs often are prepared, impassioned, and deliberate about the ventures they launch. Before taking the plunge, it would be wise to ask yourself questions such as the following:

- ◆ Have I ever balanced a budget, been involved in purchasing, or supervised accounting practices?

- Do I like managing people day in and day out?
- Have I hired and fired people? How stressful was it?
- Am I experienced in marketing and public relations?
- Does selling turn my stomach? If so, make sure you have the means to hire a top-rate sales team or you'll find yourself face to face with potential customers.
- Am I willing to work sixteen-hour or longer days to get my business off the ground?
- Do I have family support?
- Do I learn quickly on my feet? Can I react fast?
- Do I have a substantial nest egg saved for emergencies— and am I willing to dip into that to start a business or prop it up in thinner times?
- Am I comfortable networking and speaking in front of crowds?
- Am I willing to be patient for profits, many of which won't show up in the first year of operations?
- Do I want a long-term investment or a business that might be more profitable in the short term that I could more easily turn over?

If you want to explore your business acumen and likely proficiency at running your own company, the Small Business Administration offers a quick quiz on its Web site that effectively covers some of the fundamental elements an individual should possess professionally and personally to launch a successful business. You can check it out at http://www.sba.gov/gopher/Business-Development/Success-Series/Vol1/Quiz/quizall.txt. The SBA site also offers a link with specifics on how to write a business plan: http://www.sba.gov/starting_business/planning/writingplan.html.

For many people, **opening a franchise may be a relatively safe and easy challenge, thanks to the training and support of the franchisor.** Franchising entrepreneurs are buying into an established brand, training support, and proven business plans and methods as well as a perpetual pool of advisers should their business encounter operational hiccups along the way. Company managers have already conducted or investigated industry research for the line of business in which their franchise operates, not to mention geographic revenue estimates, sales strategies and earnings projections, marketing methods, management suggestions, and other business approaches that can help ensure that your particular shop is a hit with customers.

Still, launching a franchise outlet is no guarantee for success, particularly if your franchise brand isn't a household name. In a 1999 study by Scott Shane, a franchising expert and professor at the Weatherhead School of Management at Case Western Reserve University in Cleveland, Ohio, and Maw-Der Foo, a professor at the National University of Singapore, which was published in the journal *Management Science,* it was revealed that only 25 percent of new franchises whose brands were unknown lasted more than ten years.

There's much more information about franchising later in this chapter.

Top Reasons Small Businesses Fail

- ◆ Lack of experience.

- ◆ Insufficient capital (money).

- ◆ Poor location.

- ◆ Poor inventory management.

- ◆ Overinvestment in fixed assets.

- ◆ Poor credit arrangements.

- ◆ Personal use of business funds.

- ◆ Unexpected growth.

Source: Small Business Administration.

Getting Started

Know that starting a business, whether independently or through
a franchise, is a long—albeit potentially profitable and rewarding—endeavor. Franchisors, for example, may wait a year to see
their first profits. And much of what any business owner makes is
plunked right back into the company. Dreams of quick cash and
rolling in self-made money are quickly squashed by the reality of
business expenses. But don't let that deter you. The freedom, satisfaction, and inspiration of starting your own business and
watching it grow are tremendous, particularly for older workers
who have spent years in a company job dreaming of their opportunity to break out on their own.

What might be most reassuring is knowing you're not
alone. Particularly for executives who have felt the layoff pinch
of corporate axings, starting a business is more attractive today
than ever. And the Challenger, Gray & Christmas report indi-
cates that managers at all levels who launch businesses are

often well suited to do so, translating well-developed managerial skills over a career into solid management of their own enterprises.

If opening a business is definitely your calling, your next step will be figuring out what kind of business to open. The Small Business Administration suggests asking yourself a few basic questions:

◆ **What Do I Like to Do Most?** It's no secret that you'll be much happier if your business product or service is something that really inspires, interests, or motivates you. You might make a lot of money manufacturing shelving, but if it's not something that turns you on, your chance of success plummets.

◆ **What Technical Skills Do I Possess?** It's always a good idea to transfer skills you already have to a new business or job. And it will make the transition that much less intimidating if what you're doing is something you're already comfortable with.

◆ **What Do Others See as My Strong Skills?** Sometimes our greatest strengths are very apparent to our peers while they go unnoticed by us. Don't be modest. Ask anyone and everyone what they think your best skills and traits are. It might spark a whole new idea for a business.

◆ **How Much Time Do I Have or Am I Willing to Give?** This is a critical question since, if you're not willing to work countless hours—as many as twelve to sixteen a day, particularly in the first year or two of getting a business off the ground—you might as well hang it up right now. There are very few businesses that don't require intense work and commitment in the beginning. This is, again, another reason to select a business that is fascinating to you.

Got an idea of what you want to do? Great. You're on your way to getting started, but first you need to figure out if your idea is viable. Is it a business with a track record for success? What are the market fluctuations like for that industry or type of business? Basic research should start with similar businesses to determine what you can offer that they don't, what kind of success you can expect, how might you expand market offerings for that business, what growth opportunities exist in that field, and other vital considerations. And of course, once you've decided on a business idea, you'll need to think about financing, employees, taxes, equipment, insurance, office space, marketing, legalities, and other issues as you get it off the ground.

Avoiding Failure

As a former president of the international division of Mennen, Jim Farrin knows well the feeling of business success. So it was a severe wake-up call when he stumbled a couple of times with small businesses in retirement after nearly twenty years as an effective leader of a multinational company division. As the head of Snowblade in 1993, he poured his nest egg—worth hundreds of thousands of dollars—into a sled manufacturing company he launched that suffered abysmal sales in a winter with little snow. "I gave up on Snowblade," he says, but he did hold on to it long enough to recoup some of his losses in licensing fees. "One of the things you want to do at this age is put away a nest egg, not spend it. At one time we had twenty-five people in the company, and suddenly it was down to one—me."

Eighteen months later, Farrin founded Campus Clothing, a short-lived venture that manufactured graduation T-shirts for colleges and universities, printing the names of the graduating class on the back of the shirt. "It was a good concept, but we couldn't make as much money as we needed to support what we were doing." He eventually licensed the company back to the UK firm on which he'd based the initial concept.

But these business flops were by no means a loss, Farrin insists. He learned valuable lessons from them and used those mistakes to reinvigorate his post-retirement career. Now he offers programs for the American Management Association about topics such as leadership, corporate culture, and employee development. His mistakes make for valuable input that others can use to start their own businesses.

Farrin advises asking yourself: *What are my strengths and dreams? What will I be missing if I leave the corporate world to start a new venture?* Even more important, seek out an entrepreneur who has already overcome new-business hurdles. "There is no substitute for somebody who has gone through this as opposed to merely reading an article," Farrin says, "mining someone for hurdles they made and mistakes along the way."

Still, at some point opening a business comes down to simply taking the plunge. So many executives accustomed to comfortable, safe salaries and bonuses become extremely fearful when faced with the unknown, says Knauf. "Welcome to life," he adds. "You get through fear by talking about it up front and understanding that it will be part of the process."

New-business owners may take comfort in recalling other

periods in their corporate careers when they were nervous and full of anxiety about their job. Remind yourself that you got through that period, and it may help you realize that this is just another period of anxiety that can be conquered successfully.

Promotion: The Key to Success

When Marianne D'Eugenio first started her quilting shop, she made some classic marketing mistakes. She didn't have the money or faith in consultants to hire a marketing expert, but D'Eugenio admits that she was no promotional guru herself. Her natural inclination was to advertise. So she bought an ad in the local newspaper, thinking that she would grow slowly with local recognition first, since she was wary of landing too many customers at once and not being able to meet their needs. If she wanted to grow slowly, she accomplished her goal—to a fault. "Advertising in newspapers is very expensive. I was spending five hundred dollars a month for a small business-card-size ad, and I got nobody." Not exactly a resounding strategy. Her first lesson in marketing: Target the right audience. What D'Eugenio soon realized was that for her particular clientele, newspapers were far too generic a vehicle in which to advertise. She asked other retailers for their business-generating tactics. "The answer was that it was always by word of mouth, through a business card or a poster or something."

So D'Eugenio nixed the expensive newspaper campaign for quilting industry newsletters that asked only twenty-five dollars a year to place an ad. She had hundreds of business cards printed and asked visitors to the store to take one—or several—and pass them out to friends, co-workers, and family who also might be interested in quilting. Eventually those tactics created local buzz about her shop, to the point that her area newspaper wrote a story on Quadrille Quilting. "Business took off after that," she says.

If you made the move, took a leap of faith, and set up your office, congratulations. Now just sit back and wait for the phone to ring, right? Not exactly.

As D'Eugenio's story illustrates, you have to not only develop a promotional plan for your company but also devise methods to very specifically market to your target audience. It can be a daunting task that many people, if they have no experience with marketing, can find overwhelming. There are so many ways to get out the word, and a lot of inexpensive means to do so. The idea, of course, is to get the most marketing mileage out of each dollar you spend, but it can be tricky trying to figure out the venues that will garner you the most attention. A few marketing moves to keep in mind:

◆ **Make Yourself Known.** A lot of mom-and-pop shops rely on neighbors to provide them with business. But if the product or service you offer is unusual, people will come from surrounding towns, counties, even regional areas to make a purchase. Don't feel you're limited to the local market. You do have to let people know you're there, though. Make sure you're listed in directories for your industry, with your local chamber of commerce and Better Business Bureau, and with online directories—so many shoppers go online and search for options before leaving home to peruse store shelves.

◆ **Cast Your Net Wide.** As D'Eugenio's example proves, you don't want to waste money with general advertisements that shotgun a message out to a mass audience, many of whose members will skip right over your ad. On the other hand, you do want to let everyone and anyone know about your business. The key is shouting it out the right people. Tell family, friends, co-workers, and especially customers to pass along information and help get out the word about your start-up.

◆ **Spend Advertising Dollars Carefully.** When you're actually plunking down cash for ads and various marketing and promotional activities, you want to be careful what you're spending and where. If you spend thousands of dollars on newspaper or radio advertising, you may reach thousands of consumers, but if only a few trickle in as a result the return on your marketing dollars spent still leaves you in the red. Instead, look for industry publications, conferences, or networking groups where you can more directly target the audience that would be likely to need your business. **One of the best ways to gain customers is to position yourself as an expert within your industry by speaking at various events.**

◆ **Launch a Web Site.** These days, owning and operating a business without a Web site is about as effective as running a business without a phone. Finding information online has become so second nature to Americans that people are probably more likely to look up your company online as in the phone book.

◆ **Create an e-Newsletter.** Now that you've got a Web site, you need to devise methods to get people to visit that site. One of the most effective means is through e-newsletters with articles, resources, or general business information that features links back to your Web site. Something to keep in mind, however: What with spam, business correspondence, and personal e-mails, most people don't have a lot of time to read the e-mail newsletters you might send their way weekly or daily. So keep it short and sweet. Newsletters should be no more than a page, with short paragraphs or sentences that can direct readers to your Web site if they want to learn more. Include quick hits that will compel readers to link to your site, such as quick, one-question surveys.

◆ **Don't Ignore the Basics.** Having a Web presence doesn't mean that traditional methods of informing people about your business are ineffective. You should be listed in the phone book and information, because there are certainly still plenty of people who look there for business leads. And you should always have a stack of business cards on hand to hand out to every visitor. They're still one of the most effective marketing tools around—and something people carry with them everywhere. Likewise, it's smart to create stationery, notepads, and other pieces of correspondence including your name, your company's name, and its address to give people easy access to your information.

◆ **Become an Expert.** Consumers are more likely to buy from brands and business owners they have come to know and trust. If shoppers realize you are well versed in your business, they'll gravitate to your company with greater frequency. Sounds simple, but sometimes people are shy about touting their talents. Hold seminars within your industry or at an association meeting that can both showcase your knowledge and make people aware of your company. D'Eugenio did more than just open a quilting shop—she established herself as a leading teacher of the craft by offering classes to shoppers, who then saw her as an invaluable resource.

Small Businesses Resources

Clearly, starting a business isn't easy. Luckily there are some great resources out there—many of them free—for fledgling entrepreneurs.

- **SCORE,** www.score.org. The Service Corps of Retired Executives (SCORE) is a nonprofit organization that provides free online and face-to-face counseling for people starting a business. The association, founded in 1964, has 389 chapters nationwide. More than 10,000 volunteers, many former business owners themselves, have provided advice to 6.5 million aspiring entrepreneurs.

- *Inc.* **Magazine,** www.inc.com. This monthly publication's Web site provides endless free how-to articles on everything from setting up a new office to hiring and managing a sales staff. With stories that cover very simple fundamentals of operating a business, the site is particularly great for new entrepreneurs.

- *Entrepreneur* **Magazine,** www.entrepreneur.com. Similar to *Inc.* in scope, *Entrepreneur* provides loads of how-to features on various topics, from insight into the best products to sell online to marketing and management strategies. The site even includes an eBay Startup Center that walks visitors through the possibilities of creating an online auction business.

- **Small Business Administration,** www.sba.gov. The SBA has a wealth of information and tools for first-time business owners, including a Small Business Startup Guide that includes detailed instructions on how to write a business plan, among other useful tools.

- **Internal Revenue Service,** http://www.irs.gov/businesses/small/. Though it's the tax arm of the U.S. government, the IRS has a surprisingly long list of links and resources for small-business owners, providing tips and strategies on everything from employee retirement plans to avoiding business tax scams. The URL includes an online classroom with links to various small-business classes that are presented through streaming video feeds.

Franchising—The Easy Way In?

Marilyn Kendrick, fifty-six, is a franchisor's dream. She's passionate about her business, well educated to run it, and committed to her clients. She's been an owner for two years of Comfort Keepers, a national franchise that provides assisted-living services for patients in their own homes.

Kendrick made her way gradually to Comfort Keepers after becoming disillusioned with nursing in the late 1990s and fed up with it by early 2002. "I was very frustrated with the nursing practice today," Kendrick says. "I was taught to be a bedside nurse and really take care of the patients. Now you can't do that. There's a high patient load, more paperwork, and you're trying to rush out of one patient's room to get to the next one. I went home every day and didn't like what I was doing."

In addition, Kendrick and her husband moved from Oregon to Florida in 2000, where she found that full-time shifts were twelve hours long rather than the eight hours she had been accustomed to out west. And she took a nine-dollar-an-hour cut in pay. Not exactly the career move she had hoped for.

But she also realized that this wasn't her only option—her health care knowledge could lead to something else, specifically her own business. It's a plan more and more Americans are adopting as they become demoralized by stiff management in tough times, boredom with careers they aren't inspired by, or simply a need to exit the corporate world.

"One of the things that had always touched me is that I really like elderly people," Kendrick says. Indeed, when she saw elderly patients with broken hips in the hospital who were too feeble to return home and needed to be moved to nursing homes or assisted-living centers, her reaction was far more sympathetic than those of many other health care workers. "I wanted to take all those little old ladies home with me," she says, in the way an animal lover might rescue stray pets.

Eventually she did take them home, in a way, when she learned about home care franchises and decided to open her own—a branch of Comfort Keepers—in 2002. She looked at eight similar franchises, then narrowed her choices down to two, based upon the level of support, structure, and overall professional demeanor that she felt each franchise offered. Then she put down $14,500 for the franchise and another $50,000 for start-up costs.

In two years, she's grown the outfit to a three-hundred-thousand-dollar-a-year business with more than twenty clients and thirty caregivers who work in twenty-four-hour shifts. She's taught herself Microsoft Publisher, Quick Books, and methods for networking and marketing along the way. Her husband, who is a physician, helped her set up her office, which required much the same consideration as his medical office.

In addition, Kendrick received intensive training and a list of procedures to follow from Comfort Keepers that did a lot to get her business started. She spends as much as seventy hours a week working and took her first vacation in three years in September 2004, traveling through the Canadian Rockies. But the sacrifices, even later in life, have been worth it. "It was like magic when I found this," she says. "I haven't looked back or questioned it. I'm just happy I did it."

If you feel you'll need a lot of advice and help when starting your business, opening a franchise can be a safer bet than going it alone. With some three thousand franchises nationwide operating in a $625-billion-a-year industry, finding one that's interesting should be feasible. It's sifting through the ones that won't work that takes immense amounts of time, causes frustration, and can send would-be entrepreneurs hightailing it back to a nine-to-five job. But don't run so quickly. Know that finding the right franchise fit may take some time.

Companies such as Knauf's GC Alliance make their money through commissions paid by franchisors and offer free consulting services to individuals interested in opening a franchise. Other franchise consultants, including such well-known firms as Business Development Centers (www.franchise-u.com) and FranConsultant (www.franconsultant.com), work in the same way, offering free services to individuals who may want to open a franchise.

The fifty-and-over age group is the largest source of Knauf's clients, he says. They have resources, have talents developed over twenty or thirty years of working, and are often eager to get away from corporations and work for themselves. But the cautionary question, he adds, is: "Unless you've run a business before, what are the odds you know everything to start it?" There's plenty to consider:

- ◆ Location.
- ◆ Signage.
- ◆ Retail layout.

- ◆ What to sell.
- ◆ Where to find vendors.
- ◆ Distribution.
- ◆ Accounting.
- ◆ Hiring.
- ◆ Firing.
- ◆ Personnel management.
- ◆ Marketing.
- ◆ Sales.

And that's just for starters. Basically, "you have to invent that business," Knauf says. Unless you open a franchise. "The large reason why the success rate is so different [from that of individual businesses] is that when you go into a franchise, they've already done it fifty, two hundred, a thousand times. It's already invented and you don't have to create anything." Franchisors also provide training, marketing support, and key demographic information that guides owners to locations that have been researched and markets that are ripe for success.

So which franchise is for you? Start by asking yourself these questions:

- ◆ What are my business goals?
- ◆ What kind of business might motivate and inspire me day in and day out?
- ◆ What do I want to accomplish with this franchise? Do I want one shop that I'll help grow, or a series of shops within a region?
- ◆ Am I more prone to like a business with one or two employees, or would I prefer to manage a staff of at least a dozen?

◆ Am I willing to work all day, every day, or do I want to be more of a hands-off owner? That's rarely an option, by the way, even with franchises. At least in the beginning, nearly every franchise owner needs to be on site to make sure business is operating smoothly, managers are supervising staff appropriately, and company employees aren't taking advantage of your absence. One franchisee with Panera Bread was a former executive who now finds himself in the store as early as 6 AM kneading dough for the day's sandwiches and baked goods. If that's not your cup of tea, get out now. Franchises rarely offer bankers' hours or even eight-hour workdays.

◆ Do I plan on operating my franchise for years to come or just for the next five to seven?

Don't just look at the big names like Burger King, which can require an investment upward of four hundred thousand dollars to start. Plenty of lucrative franchises can be launched for half that or less. In fact, Knauf cautions his clients against opening the first franchises that come to mind—those that they visit or drive by themselves every day. Instead, branch out. You never know what franchise you might hit upon that's perfect for you, and looking at a lot of different ones—rather than the one McDonald's you're sure will be a cash cow—allows you to take a look at how other companies operate regarding contracts, royalties, territories, franchisor expectations, and other issues. Plus, **having a household name doesn't guarantee success.** And even if it does, too many people launch well-known brands and make money, but hate the business they run.

Make sure you know what you're getting into financially, too. A woman called Knauf recently after she spotted a 250-seat microbrewery franchise in her town. "She said, 'I'd like to open that,'" Knauf recalls. "I said, great, tell me about your financials." About $250,000 was what the woman had to offer.

"I said, here lies the problem," Knauf continues. "'That restaurant cost twelve million dollars to build.' She didn't say a whole lot other than, 'It's not much bigger than my house.' I said, 'You have a point, but your home probably doesn't have a walk-in cooler that could hold your neighborhood.'"

The lesson: Know your franchise costs. Restaurants, for example, tend to generate low profit margins.

Sources for Franchise Information

Want to start a franchise but you have no clue where to begin? Thankfully, the idea is so popular there are a plethora of Web sites out there to help, not to mention services that provide face-to-face consultations:

♦ **The International Franchise Association,** www.franchise.org, is the membership organization for franchisors, franchisees, and suppliers—essentially a one-stop shop for everything a person could want to know about franchising as well as a robust resource for contacts and education.

♦ **Franchise.com,** www.franchise.com. This group was created to encourage and provide franchising opportunities around the world. You can browse available franchises by country or try the Web site's "franchise matchmaker" to assess which brand may be best for you.

♦ **The Franchise Handbook,** www.franchisehandbook.com. The site claims to have the most comprehensive and up-to-date database of franchises available. That may or may not be true, but the compilation you'll find is seemingly endless. Other information is also available, and very helpful, such as links to sites with legal forms for franchising and message boards for visitors.

♦ **Franchise Opportunities,** www.franchiseopportunities.com, offers a unique list of franchises ranked by opportunity—platinum, gold, and silver. AAMCO, for example, is among the list of platinum contenders, while 7-Eleven ranks as gold.

♦ **Franchise Chat,** www.franchise-chat.com. Stumped by a franchise question that you need someone to answer? You might find out quickly at Franchise Chat, which was created with two objectives in mind: to serve as an Internet resource for people who are considering becoming or have already become franchisees, and to provide a forum for open discussions about franchising. The site gets thousands of visitors from thirty different countries.

♦ **FranNet,** www.frannet.com, provides free franchising consulting services, research, testimonials, and in-person appointments for those who want to meet with a consultant face to face. The site also provides tips on what to consider when exploring franchises and links to other sites, such as SCORE.

♦ **FranChoice,** www.franchoice.com. Also offering free franchise consultations, FranChoice's site is clean and easy to navigate and provides helpful tools such as a franchise aptitude self-test you can take to determine your likelihood of successfully operating a franchise.

♦ ***Franchise UPDATE* Magazine,** www.franchise-update.com. It's always a good idea to peruse the trade publications of any business or industry you plan to work in. *Franchise UPDATE* provides profiles of people and franchises as well as information on franchising conferences.

Becoming a Consultant

Becoming a consultant after twenty or more years in a particular field seems a natural step. But it's not as easy as propping your feet on the desk in the home office and waiting for the phone to ring. Robert Cannon, of Cannon Advantage, discovered that when he opened his business consultancy in 2001 at the age of fifty-four after he "traded in the wood-paneled office on executive row for an office at home and the corporate jet for the trusty family car." There are days when he feels business is bone-dry, and others when "you feel you have more than you can handle," he says.

The client roller coaster can be unnerving, but the experience has been worth it, according to Cannon. "I'd gotten to the point where I'd been in sales and marketing for thirty years and in the executive ranks for twenty, including having served on boards and a variety of other things. I thought, *I don't want to go back and do the same things over again. I want to do different things and grow as a person.*"

His consultancy has led him toward business he would never have considered otherwise. Part of that has been driven by a need to expand his skills. Through a class in appreciative inquiry at Case Western Reserve University, he learned a new management method that uses collaboration to engage people and facilitate change within companies. An early experience in which he led a post-9/11 discussion among Muslims, Jews, Hare Krishnas, Protestants, and Catholics on what a collaborative future between the groups could look like made him realize that his consulting business could be expanded to far more than the corporate arena.

The cost of launching his consulting practice was somewhere in the neighborhood of fifty thousand dollars—seven thousand for classes, and the rest spent to launch a Web site; print stationery, brochures, and business cards; attend industry seminars; and set up a home office complete with furniture, equipment, and other necessary business tools. His practice is worth $110,000 today, a value he's not entirely pleased with, but it's a growing practice and the lifestyle it affords him is unprecedented, he says. "I can work as long as I want and do it for me for a change."

Setting Up Your Office

For his business, Cannon finds that working out of his home makes sense. After all, he can't beat the thirty-second commute. Other consultants find renting space more helpful. But it can be a tough call. On the one hand, if client meetings are a big part of your sales process, it may not always be possible to meet in customers' offices. And talking shop over a latte at the local Starbucks may not fill your prospect with overwhelming confidence. On the other, don't jump into a lease that can add significantly to the costs of your consulting business when you don't need to. Setting up a home office is much cheaper—something that can be done with as little as a few thousand dollars. What's more, plenty of million-dollar businesses had their beginnings in basements or garages. If a home office is your route, consider the following to optimize your house's space and prime working conditions:

◆ **Designate Space.** It's key to allot a specific area of your home for work—preferably something other than the unused corner of your second bedroom. It may seem idyllic in the beginning of your home business to literally roll out of bed and into work, but a year from now you'll be wishing the "office" were a little more official. Try to at least section off a room or area of your house that can be exclusively used for work purposes. It should be large enough for a desk, a comfortable chair, any computer, fax, and printing equipment you need, file cabinets, and other business necessities, such as a small copy machine. And try to keep family and personal items out of that space so that it's a working area only. Also, experts almost universally insist that ample light is key to enjoying your work space. If your basement is truly the best place to set up shop, but it's dark, just make sure you're prepared to light it up as needed.

◆ **Organize Relentlessly.** You'll find your entrée into self-employment much easier if you keep things organized. File everything back in its place at the end of the day, and add an above-desk bookshelf if necessary if you don't already have enough space. You don't have to hire a carpenter; you can buy materials at the Home Depot and build shelves from scratch. Very cheap organizational products and ideas can be found at places like the Container Store, where freestanding shelving starts as low as sixty dollars.

◆ **Don't Mix Family (or Pets) and Work.** It's not a sin to have your faithful Labrador by your feet as you work, but you'd better hope he doesn't start barking in the middle of a client call. Separation of family and business should be maintained right down to the phone line. It's unprofessional to have kids picking up your business line—and potentially a liability as well if they tie up the phone while you're waiting for important clients to call. Likewise, depending on how busy your phone and fax lines are, you may want to dedicate separate lines for both so customers aren't frustrated with busy signals when they call.

◆ **Keep the Peace.** One New York journalist lived and worked on one of the city's busiest streets and was constantly straining to hear interview subjects when fire engines and police cars blared past her windows on the street below—something that occurred as often as ten times a day. Consider external noises—neighbors, area construction, traffic—that may be audible for customers who call.

◆ **Back Yourself Up.** Now that you're on your own, there's no information technology department to come to the rescue when you lose a file. Back up your work weekly, if not daily—a good investment is an external Zip drive, which can be purchased for less than a hundred dollars.

◆ **Don't Be Chintzy on Furniture.** Now that you're making the office-furniture-buying decisions rather than your company's purchasing department, you can cut costs on desks and other needed equipment substantially. One thing *not* to skimp on: the office chair. It's probably the most important piece of work equipment you'll own, and the level of comfort it provides can vastly impact your level of productivity. That doesn't mean you should run out and blow fifteen hundred bucks on a Herman Miller masterpiece. But it does mean you shouldn't transfer one of your hard-backed dining room chairs to your office and stiffen up your back every day. You can find phenomenal deals on great chairs at outlets such as Office Depot and Staples, or low-cost home furniture stores like Ikea.

Chapter 7

Women in the Workplace

This year, Antoinette Kuritz will host the fourth meeting of the group she founded: the La Jolla Writer's Conference in San Diego, an annual gathering of budding authors and established writers who provide insight, advice, and inspiration to aspiring writers. A fifty-five-year-old literary publicist, Kuritz has seen her event grow from nothing to two hundred attendees a year (her maximum number of allowed guests). In addition, she hosts the weekly *Writer's Roundtable* radio program on Internet radio station World Talk Radio, averaging five thousand listeners a show.

It hasn't all come easy. In fact, it's taken years of intense struggle and self-doubt for Kuritz to transform herself from a stay-at-home mom to a nationally recognized publicist and writing expert.

The idea of reentering the workplace after being away for ten or fifteen years can be intimidating at the least, and downright terrifying for some. "I think anyone entering an activity they have not been involved in before or for a long time would naturally have feelings about whether it's the right thing to do,

136

whether they're any good at it, whether it's too hard, whether people will look at them funny," says Shelley MacDermid, director of the Purdue University Center for Families in Lafayette, Indiana. The key to overcoming their fears: remembering "they're not alone," MacDermid says. "Everybody in a work site feels insecure and uncertain about something."

For Kuritz, it was the idea of reentering a work world she had become unfamiliar with and detached from after more than a decade spent raising her children. Aside from an occasional substitute teaching assignment or longer-term teaching stint, Kuritz virtually never worked outside the home. Then a freak accident happened while pumping gas one day. The handle of the pump she had used broke off after she backed up her car, freeing the gasoline hose, which fell to the ground and whipped around wildly "like a garden hose run amok" says Kuritz, dousing her in gasoline when she got near it. The resulting injuries were devastating and chronic. "My tear ducts were burned out so my eyes were always itchy and swollen. Gas infections showed up all over my body, and I had lead all in my blood," Kuritz says. "I developed asthma and was only breathing at 35 percent" capacity; she also suffered short-term memory loss. Kuritz's own doctors failed to believe that gasoline could be so physically destructive, even if a person had been saturated in the liquid. And "there were all these doctors from the gasoline company who would say, 'Gasoline doesn't do this to you.'"

Maybe not, but Kuritz experienced physical debilitation and, consequently, serious depression. Finally, when it seemed no doctor would ever help, she decided she'd had enough. Now that her children were grown, she needed a distraction that would refocus her mind on something other than her failing health. Work, she thought, had to be it. She'd always loved books, so she decided to apply for a job as a "lowly bookstore employee." She got the position—and a paltry salary of $4.85 an hour. But Kuritz was in the right spot and she knew it. She loved books, and her new job was indeed pulling her mind away from her physical ailments.

Kuritz realized something else as well: Her inherent passion for reading was naturally and organically fueling her professional ambitions. Within six months, she'd pushed time and again to be the community relations coordinator who hosted book readings for authors with new works and other events for area residents. Finally, she got the job. Her salary jumped to only $6.50 an hour, but Kuritz found immense value in what she was doing professionally.

Her first event was, by all accounts, a disaster: Only two people showed up. But that was because the last in a long line of community relations directors to be fired had done nothing to promote the event. Kuritz stood before the authors featured that night in tears, promising that their next event would attract at least 125 people. The authors reassured her that their little-known works didn't draw crowds anyway. But Kuritz was convinced otherwise, and she kept her promise to those authors by devising a unique interactive mystery game during their next reading that she heavily promoted in local newspapers and within the store. "The two authors came back and we stopped counting attendees at 125," Kuritz says.

It was the boost that her career needed. Similarly successful events followed one after the other, and Kuritz, her reputation as a great promoter now established, was eventually recruited to another bookstore, where she upped her pay, albeit nominally, and was first approached by an author to become a publicist. Perhaps still held back by her uncertainty about her talents, she was hesitant at first. But this particular author agreed to replace her current salary in full so she could quit her bookstore job and focus exclusively on promoting his books. She agreed and, one by one, slowly began to build a very respectable reputation taking on other authors through referrals. It's led to a successful career that now pays well over six figures a year.

To be certain, a lot of extenuating circumstances were working in Kuritz's favor. She happened to land a job in a bookstore where the community relations coordinators simply weren't creative—multiple times in a row—opening the door for Kuritz. At the time she held that position, community events were viewed as a premium and the store's budget, which was substantially heftier than it is now, allowed Kuritz to execute some unusual programs that required more preparation and money. But her real success, Kuritz would argue, happened because a series of events and opportunities flowed naturally from her passion for what she did and the hard work she put in, which grabbed people's attention and made them take notice. And she would be right.

Luck and circumstance do play a role in every successful career, but there's usually one other critical factor in success: dedication to what you do. That's good news for women reentering the labor market after years away—or for women who currently work but are eager to explore new options. If you have the determination to succeed, there's no reason that you can't. If, however, you pin your chances on hope and luck—well, you may come up empty-handed.

As for having the nerve to return to work in the first place after so many years away raising kids, Kuritz insists that the key was finding employment grounded in a lifetime passion—in her case, reading. It's what helped her get through moments when neighbors and friends within the community were too embarrassed to speak to a mere bookstore clerk. "It's humbling and demeaning. Here I am working at a local bookstore pushing around a cart. Friends would walk in and look at me and walk to another aisle," she recalls.

But as Kuritz's career blossomed and she began promoting more and more authors, those same women came back to seek out Kuritz and her promotional skills along with her author contacts for community fund-raisers. Kuritz doesn't begrudge them their fickleness, but rather chalks such experiences up to paying her professional dues during a "five-year bookstore boot camp"—a way to reestablish herself after so many years of not working, in order to achieve her ultimate career goals.

As Kuritz proves, being absent from the workforce for years doesn't mean you're obsolete to corporate America. The key is to know what you have to offer and how to effectively present that to potential employers. Being a mother is hard work, and a tremendous arena for skill development. "A lot they've learned as mothers can be valuable in the workplace," MacDermid says. "They know what it means to be dependable, committed, get a lot of different things done at once."

Women at Work

Just because you decided to hang up full-time motherhood doesn't mean you have to go full steam ahead and jump back into a sixty-hour-a-week job on Wall Street. Likewise for career women who are bored, frustrated, or otherwise stagnating in their current professional roles, there is a vast array of opportunities for women looking to shift their position within the workplace. In fact, trying an atypical work schedule that provides a little free time in your daily routine may not only make a career transition less anxiety-ridden but also build your enthusiasm for taking on more work and responsibility in the process. Think about the following options:

◆ **Full-Time Work.** If you are a mom and returning to full-time work is what you're after, by all means go for it. So many women are finding themselves and their careers rejuvenated later in life as they get back into the swing of a full-time work life. Many are realizing that they can still have a rich career and be grateful that they spent the years they did at home with their families. Just take a few moments before making the plunge to realize what *full time* means to you. Is it thirty-five hours a week, forty hours, or more than fifty? And make sure the employer you're interviewing with has the same definition you do.

◆ **Temporary Work.** Temp work is always a good way to test the waters and determine what kind of office environment you may enjoy best, to learn the kinds of work you might want to explore, and simply to gain the feeling of being back in the workplace or in a different work environment. It's also a golden opportunity to get some free training in things like software programs, which many staffing firms offer their workers for free. Ask about what computer training they offer and if they have any limitations on what programs you can receive training on.

◆ **Part-Time Work.** If you're a stay-at-home mom and still tepid on the idea of going back to work, particularly full time, part-time work can be a good way to get your feet wet and see which type of work environment or line of employment suits you best. This is also a good arrangement for those mothers whose children haven't quite left the nest. This way you can fulfill, at least in part, your employment interests and still have time for your kids.

◆ **Internships.** If you're concerned that your skill development is still ongoing, or your experience (or lack thereof) may hold you back, internships are a great way to land a quality work experience and prove just how valuable you are. But it's important once you land an internship to make the most of it. And you'll likely have to take the initiative, since interns can sometimes be forgotten if they don't speak up and make themselves noticed. Walk around when you're not busy and introduce yourself to other staff members. Ask about their jobs, other people they may know in the industry, helpful job-hunting tips they may have, and so on. Be careful not to hound your co-workers, however. You want to leave an impression that you're earnest, eager, and conscientious about your potential new line of work. But you don't want to seem like someone who runs around the firm nagging co-workers for job leads.

◆ **Work at Home.** It seems ironic, since the whole idea is to actually *get out* of the house that you've spent so much time in for the past ten or twenty years, but setting up a business at home can offer both income and the satisfaction of work while still allowing you the flexibility to raise children who may be at home. It's a way to create your own work schedule and not be pinned down by the rigid hours of corporate jobs. If you do open a home business, though, make sure you set aside plenty of hours for it. The last thing you want is to have your business sabotaged inadvertently by family members who are constantly around, making it difficult for you to get your work done.

◆ **Job Sharing.** This can be a great solution for women who want to work but not full time, for those in a career transition who need more time to explore other types of jobs, and for those who still want to keep a hand in their home life a few days a week. If you're reentering the workforce and looking for a high-powered job, chances are slim to none that a company will offer job sharing right off the bat. But certain industries, including the service professions, are open to such work arrangements. Or, if you work for a few years full time and prove your worth, you might be able to negotiate a job-sharing opportunity.

◆ **Contract Work.** This is usually reserved for people with specific skills, who are hired to complete a project in which those skills are needed—a great opportunity for women who are looking to explore employment options. Plenty of project and interim work is available, and it can offer a nice juxtaposition of full-time employment followed by a chunk of time off—or not, depending on how quickly the next project follows and how soon you want to get back to work.

Back in the Game

If you left work to raise children years ago, before you even decide to reenter the work world, you should make sure it's what you really want to do. Think about your needs professionally now versus twenty years ago:

- ◆ Are you still as motivated by work now as you were when you left the workplace? Does the corporate ladder still beckon, or is work the second time around more about having a hand and sense of ownership in a professional project rather than overall career prestige and position?
- ◆ Are you willing to go back to school if that's what it takes to gain the skills you need to reenter your old career or launch a new one?
- ◆ Is your family prepared for this? Have you talked to them about your time away from the home and what that means for them? The number of hours you'll be working? The fact that you may have to skip a soccer tournament here or there? On the other side, have you had an honest conversation with yourself about how much you'll miss all that when you return to work?

- How many hours a week do you want to work? Is full-time employment or part-time work the answer for you?
- Are you prepared for the worst a career can deliver: Office politics? Negative reviews? Nasty co-workers? Sexist peers?

So you think you're ready for all that? Great. It's a plunge that can offer great rewards and satisfaction later in life—the ultimate experience of having your cake and eating it, too, now that you've been able to devote two decades to your children and still seek professional satisfaction.

Like any older workers launching into a new career, however, mothers returning to the workplace need to explore some key considerations before beginning a job search. Most basic: Do you want a job or a career? "There is a clear, important distinction," says Nancy Collamer, a career consultant and founder of JobsAndMoms.com, an online resource for mothers looking to go back to work. "Are you just looking for something that will get you out of the house and bring in a paycheck where you can leave at 5 PM every day? You really want to spend some time being honest with yourself about that."

Figure out that first question and the next one naturally follows: What do you want to do? Stumped? There are plenty of free services to help moms—and women making a shift mid-career—figure this out, from condensed and full-scale versions of the famous Myers-Briggs personality test online to free or low-cost community workshops. Local unemployment offices also offer a wealth of free information and resources as well as dozens of job listings. Or check your local YWCA for career development programs—some can run less than a hundred dollars.

If you've worked before, an easy way to start the process may be to make a pros-and-cons list for every job you've ever held. If you haven't worked, write down any community or volunteer work you might have done. Underneath each job, list what responsibilities, tasks, and job elements you loved and hated. You might want to rank them in order of appeal if that helps. Look at the patterns of likes and dislikes that develop and start exploring jobs that meet those needs.

Most experts agree that **it's easier to reenter the job market through a company or industry you've worked in before.** But if you're a mom returning to work and you disliked your previous position, that doesn't mean you have to get stuck in the same job, Collamer insists. If you like the industry in which you worked but not the last position you held, "it's a whole lot easier to switch" jobs within the same industry than to enter a new one entirely. That holds true for currently employed women looking to embark on a new job search. "To switch both the job title and the industry and do something totally different is unrealistic if you're not willing to start at the bottom." Then again, if you really want to follow your passion, that may be the way to do it. It certainly was for Sharai Rudolphi. For twenty years, she was a stay-at-home mom. But after her husband became so ill that Rudolphi wasn't sure he would live, she began to consider what her future would look like. And finances were a big concern. She would most likely have to go back to work, but "I didn't want to be flipping burgers," she says. Still, with a hodgepodge of past work experience as a waitress, retail clerk, secretary, model, and sign painter, Rudolphi, now fifty-four, wasn't sure if carving out a career was possible.

She decided to enroll in human services classes at her local community college, made easier by a relearner's program at the school that helps older students transition back into the academic setting and figure out a course of study. "I had insecurities about my age," Rudolphi admits. "It's scary to be in your fifties and not be sure if you can make it. Plus, you don't fit in with the eighteen-year-olds."

Her efforts paid off. She received her associate's degree at fifty-one. Practicum work during school in a women's domestic violence shelter led to a part-time job with the organization, at twenty hours per week. In August 2004, she was promoted to a full-time position as a child specialist, teaching mothers and children with challenging backgrounds how to live more productive lives.

The path Rudolphi took was a smart one, simply because nonprofit organizations are often easier to penetrate and can be more flexible for moms who don't want to take on full-time work. Education systems offer the same opportunities. Teachers are always in demand, and substitute teaching offers a way to earn cash while you decide if that's a career you'd like to pursue further with additional schooling for a teaching certificate. Schools can be sources of jobs other than teaching as well. One of Collamer's former clients left her position at an ad agency for a couple of years to stay at home. During that time, she got involved with a new area school, became the PTA president, and eventually was hired to be the communications director for the school system—a job that tapped her advertising background to some degree. The best part: "She gets to work until 4 PM," says Collamer, who adds that other fields like health care offer entry points for returning moms that massive corporations don't feel obligated to offer.

Regaining Your Skills

In an ideal world, as a stay-at-home mom you would have raised your kids but kept your hand in some form of work over the years. Maybe you were formerly a teacher and you maintained a substitute teaching role a few weeks a year just to keep your experience current in the classroom. But not everyone has that luxury.

If you need to establish some work experience fast, the best way to do so may be volunteering. But skip the local bake sale where your greatest responsibility will probably be to whip up your best batch of chocolate fudge brownies. Such events are great fund-raisers and are sorely needed, but the responsibility level they demand is rarely impressive to a corporate recruiter.

Instead, look for volunteering positions at local chapters of national organizations, if you can. Most cities have a National Cancer Society or American Heart Association office, for example, in which area residents can offer to get involved with community events, fund-raisers, or volunteer services within the office. Organizations of this size generally have more widespread and higher levels of responsibility in which you can experience being part of something that raises hundreds of thousands of dollars or coordinates the efforts of hundreds of people—noteworthy, high-level tasks that would impress any HR professional.

When Rudolphi went back to school and later landed her first work in a domestic violence shelter, it was through volunteering. But her credentials even to get that harked back to community volunteerism she did while her children were growing up. Some of it was "fluffy," as Rudolphi says, but other volunteer work through her church included more sophisticated tasks, such as creating a children's curriculum for the assembly and organizing fund-raising Christmas drives for disadvantaged inner-city mothers and children—a perfect complement to the skill set she would be developing at the shelter. So when it was time to go back to school and launch her career, Rudolphi had a base of skills from which to build and a good idea of what she was already skilled at.

Going back to school is certainly a quick way to update your skills and become comfortable with talents that might have become rusty. Be wary of getting in too deep financially, however. Degree programs may be necessary if, say, you want to become a therapist or accountant, but some jobs, such as those in the computer industry, simply require certifications or a brush-up on new skills. You don't want to pour too much money into schooling if you don't need to. And even a class or two will put you in touch with instructors who can serve as a link to other contacts and job leads in your profession.

One thing to consider when going back to school: There's a better chance than not that you will be older than your fellow students by a good fifteen or twenty years. It pays to try to relate to them on their level. After all, you may be seeing more of them in the workplace someday. That doesn't mean you should bleach your hair, pierce your belly button, and throw on a pair of low-rise jeans as you head to campus. But don't assume that students half your age are too young for you to relate to, either.

Aging expert and author Jeri Sedlar recalls a humorous incident in which a forty-four-year-old woman, who went back to school to get a master of fine arts degree at New York University, was tripped up by a simple generational reference. One day the woman approached a group of much younger students and started chatting with them. One of the students asked her what month Kennedy died. Naturally the woman thought back to November 1963, when President John F. Kennedy was shot while riding in his motorcade. The students looked at her as if she were crazy, until they all realized they were talking about different Kennedys, the students trying to pinpoint the death of John Kennedy Jr., whose plane crashed in July 1999 off the coast of Massachusetts.

That's not a big deal, but it is an indication that generation gap miscues can happen in the office. "We have a tendency to put things through our filter," Sedlar says. "Mature workers have to think about those current benchmarks."

Along those same lines, older workers need to consider how the office environment and culture will have changed since they left. How you dress, behave, and appear to your co-workers on your first day back can significantly affect how well you transition back into the workplace. Nobody likes to hear anything as superficial as *Looks matter,* but in the business world, they do. More important, it's a good idea to find out the proper work attire for your particular office. A small Web company may not care if people come to work in shorts, while larger firms may require suits or at least casual business attire. You don't want to be under- or overdressed wherever you end up working.

Keys to Job Hunting

If you've been home with your kids, or had your nose buried in work within the same organization for years, you've probably lost that knack for what it takes to conduct a successful job search. Reviewing the cover letter and résumé-writing tips in chapter 3 might be a good idea. You might also try starting with these crucial steps:

◆ **Do Your Homework.** Since stay-at-home moms often haven't been in the workforce for years, and thus may have lost track of the latest developments in their field, getting reacquainted with industry trends, news, market developments, and key players should be first on their agenda. Likewise, women in one industry looking to transfer to another—or even to a different position within the same market—should check out trade magazines, related area conferences, and consultants or experts in their line of work. If any friends, neighbors, fellow church members, or other people in your community work in your field of interest, take them to lunch and ask them about their job, industry, expected pay, and other information you may be looking for. You'll need all of that and more when you finally land your first interview.

◆ **Understand the Job.** Applying for a specific job? Make sure you understand the exact skill set the job demands. That way you can focus your résumé and the experiences you've had out of the workplace to show how you meet the position's needs. How? Most companies will offer a job description to applicants. If not, ask for one. Once you have one, look up the job title in sources, such as the *Occupational Outlook Handbook* (produced every two years by the Department of Labor to describe working conditions, necessary training, educational requirements, pay, and expected job prospects for various occupations), to find out more. Peruse other similar titles online in job Web sites, or even try plugging the title into Google, which will likely pull up thousands of results for jobs with the same title and descriptions of responsibilities.

◆ **Volunteering Speaks Volumes.** Think community work doesn't hold its own against corporate experience? Think again. Many volunteering jobs are just as demanding as work within the private sector. And it's a rich area moms can tap to showcase their abilities when presenting themselves in an interview. "If you participated in a bake sale, that's not going to get you very far," Collamer says. "But if you were the chairperson for a major gala that raised two hundred thousand dollars, that is very impressive." Jeri Sedlar recalls one woman who was told by admissions administrators that she got into graduate school at Harvard largely because of the challenges she faced and overcame as the treasurer of her college sorority. She detailed those challenges in her application and ended up impressing the admissions staff with her ingenuity. You never know what will catch someone's attention.

♦ **Get Up to Speed.** In the event that the position you're interested in does require some additional knowledge of software programs, for example, or certification of some type, look into that before applying for the job so you can at least tell the company rep conducting the interview that you're aware of the skills needed and have already begun to acquire them. Be careful of how much time and money you dump into a potential career, however. Keep an eye out for inexpensive ways—such as continuing education classes at a local college—to quickly get up to speed on your profession without dropping a bundle.

♦ **Tap Every Resource.** Perusing the Sunday want ads is a start—but certainly not the only thing you should be doing to conduct a smart job search. Want people to know you're available for work? Then tell everyone and anyone, from neighbors to community acquaintances to contacts in training programs and local workshops. Try joining local networking groups or associations related to your industry that might provide networking opportunities and job contacts.

♦ **Think Globally, Start Locally.** Don't think your first job back in has to be the last. If you've been out of the workplace for a while, or are transitioning to a new career from your current one, there's a good chance you're not qualified for an upper- or even midlevel position. **The key is to seek out jobs that will be good stepping-stones to the next.** "Even if it's not the perfect job, it's a way to get some experience and get into the routine of working again," says

Collamer. Show a lot of ambition, work hard, and chances are that the job will be a springboard to something more rewarding and lucrative. And don't rule out small, even very small, businesses— they're often the ones that will take a chance on a new job candidate when a corporate behemoth won't. And they are far more likely to be open to alternative work schedules.

Negotiating Your Salary

Sad to say, since you've left the working world gender gaps in salaries haven't changed much. For women still in the work world, that's a painful reality. Women working full time still earn less than their male counterparts—24 percent less on average according to the 2003 salary survey conducted by the National Association of Female Executives, which compared salaries in twenty-one business sectors.

There are a lot of reasons and theories about why women miss out on larger salaries—lack of mentors, insider office networks, gender discrimination, and their own reticence to speak up for higher wages, among others. Add to that the fact that you've been off the market for a decade or more and it's clear that you need to have some sharp negotiating skills as you angle for a worthy salary.

If you're reentering work through an entry-level position, there may not be a lot of leeway in how much a company can pay you. Many of these jobs offer nonnegotiable salaries. But if your position is of a middle- or upper-level managerial rank, you definitely have some room to discuss what's appropriate. Just be prepared before you do so. Know how much you actually need, for starters, to pay your bills, then decide how much

you want to ask for and how much you would be willing to settle for. A good way to land on those figures? Check the Bureau
of Labor Statistics (www.bls.gov) for median salaries within
your field; job board Web sites list figures as well. One easy site
for information is salary.com. And to back up that requested
salary, have a prepared list of reasons for why you deserve it—
such as your accomplishments, prior salary history, skill level,
and potential value as an employee.

Even if your ideal salary doesn't come through, don't despair.
You may still have some negotiating wiggle room, but in the
area of flexibility—leaving early for a child's sporting event, for
example.

Easing Back into Work

If it's a little daunting to jump whole hog back into the workplace, you might try to do it in stages. Think of it as a form of
reverse phasing, the tactic that so many retirees are using to exit
their careers. Start with part-time or interim work. Temporary
agencies are always a good job source, as are internships in the
field you're interested in. Both allow a brief look into an industry, office, or company. Better to find out that you hate account
management during an internship at an ad agency than to spend
months interviewing only to finally land a job and realize it's not
for you. Moreover, don't forget that staffing agencies frequently
provide free training for their temporary employees—a huge
benefit to increasing your desirability in the job market.

There's also the possibility of working from home, and a slew
of Web sites have popped up in recent years dedicated to helping
stay-at-home moms participate in this increasingly popular

form of work. Plenty of businesses—from franchises to home-grown enterprises—can be set up from home. They include everything from dog training to dance instruction, and they offer mothers a way to get back to work but still be around for their children.

A cynic might dismiss *at-home worker* as just another term for "freelancer" or "free agent." But the benefit of categorizing mothers in this specific group is that so many Web sites have been developed—largely by other stay-at-home moms in similar situations—to help women navigate that transition. Just a small sampling of sites that offer tips, networking, and support for setting up businesses or working at home includes the following:

◆ **SBA Online Women's Business Center,** www.onlinewbc.gov. Sponsored by the Small Business Administration, this site focuses solely on women's concerns in regard to starting businesses and offers general information about starting a business as well as links to mentors, local SBA offices, and other resources.

◆ **Home-Based Working Moms,** www.hbwm.com. This site was started in 1995 by a stay-at-home mom who wanted to work but also wanted to continue to spend time with her children. The site includes a kit for figuring out the at-home business for you and includes tips on child care, figuring your expenses, and how to promote your home-grown business, among other things.

◆ **Internet Based Moms,** www.internetbasedmoms.com, serves as a great social, professional, and networking conduit for moms who work from home and particularly for those who run Web-based companies. Articles on the site cover topics such as Internet marketing and small-business bookkeeping.

◆ **Unlimited Mom,** www.unlimitedmom.com, is really geared more toward mothers who choose to continue their careers as they enter motherhood. Still, it's a good source of materials for older moms who return to work but may have children at home.

◆ **Work At Home Moms,** www.wahm.com. A whimsical, conversational site, Work At Home Moms (WAHM) is dedicated to creating an online community for mothers who set up businesses at home. The site includes periodic, lighthearted columns on the happenings of stay-at-home moms who work as well as classified ads, an advice columnist, telecommuting job listings, message boards, and state-by-state listings for other WAHM members who can be contacted in your area.

◆ **Moms Network,** www.momsnetwork.com. A hodgepodge of advice, resources, and job listings, this site packs in just about everything that a stay-at-home mom could need to work from home. The site offers worthwhile services, too, such as free e-mail, newsletters, links to a host of other sites, and the opportunity to connect with other women working at home. Membership is free; the site currently has more than twenty-six hundred members.

◆ **Moms Expo,** www.momsexpo.com. The site's tagline, "The web site where stay-at-home moms become work-at-home moms," just about sums it up. This well-organized and easy-to-navigate site offers message boards, a resource library, networking programs, and a sales directory, among other things.

Home Business Trends

Need an idea for a home business? The following ideas are featured on the Small Business Administration's online Women's Business Center as growing trends for home businesses. See one you think sounds appealing? Just make sure you are truly interested in it and not simply adopting it as your home business because you think glomming onto a trend is the key to business success. To be involved enough to make a business work, you have to feel impassioned about the product or service you are selling. Below, some popular ideas:

- Calendar service.

- Cleaning services.

- Employee trainer.

- Errand service.

- Expert services broker.

- Facialist.

- Family child care provider.

- Fitness trainer.

- Indoor environmental tester.

- In-home health care.

- Professional organizer.

- Mediator.

- Mystery shopper.

- Pet-sitter.

- Plant care giver.

- Professional practice consultant.

- Referral service.

- Reunion planner.

- Rubber stamp business.

- Security consultant.

- Special events planner.

- Specialized temporary agency.

- Wedding consultant.

- Wedding makeup artist.

Source: SBA Women's Business Center/Top Home-Based Business Trends Report.

Balancing Work and Family

If you're a mom returning to the office, your decision to head back to the workforce is a monumental change for both you and your family. And their support of your choice to return to work can't be underestimated. But it's important to realize that **every family member's life will be thrown into the equation.** Kids don't stop needing homework help, rides to school, and your support in general in their everyday lives.

So your decision to return to work affects them as much as it does you. Before deciding to return to the office, sit down with your family and talk about life changes that will no doubt occur: financial changes, time commitments, increased stress within the household, and other considerations. Above all else, don't expect to be supermom. "In some families, the marital agreement is, 'If you want to go back to work, that's great as long as it doesn't disrupt things here,'" MacDermid says.

That kind of thinking will end disastrously for everyone, she adds. All parties—husband, wife, kids—need to find common ground about what Mom's successful return to work will mean to the family and how everyone can pitch in to make that happen. "There needs to be a realistic discussion about how things will change and a negotiation about who can do what, so Mom isn't left feeling like she has the weight of the world on her shoulders on top of a paying job," MacDermid says.

Trial runs of what it's like for Mom to be absent from the family household might be a wise idea before she starts her job. Take day trips away from the house to mimic what life will be like when you're not there in your role as a stay-at-home mom. If young children are in day care and Mom used to pick them up, then those parents who are still married need to have a discussion about how Dad can help out with picking up kids and helping fill in on other daily tasks that Mom might once have done on her own. A mother's choice to go back to work has implications for everyone in the family, MacDermid insists. And "everyone in the family has to be a part of making it happen."

Reorienting the Family

When stay-at-home moms return to work, there may be a period of adjustment for family members, not the least of which may be moms battling guilt, nervousness about working again, and anxiety about how all these changes are going to play out at home. All of that is natural, but you don't have to just suffer through it without relief. There are certainly ways to make the transition easier:

◆ **Have a Family Powwow.** No point in beating around the bush. Sit down with your family—perhaps your spouse first—and have a heart-to-heart about how everyone feels about you returning to work, what that may mean for the kids, and how important it is for you to rejoin the labor market.

◆ **Reorganize Workloads.** You can try to be a supermom and drive yourself insane, or you can reshift household expectations and responsibilities. With you back at work, even if it's part time, you'll have less time to attend to your normal routine around the house and community. If kids need to cook meals because you'll be late one night or find alternate transportation home from swim practice, establish all the scheduling changes and resolutions up front. That way no one's caught off guard and chaos and resentment don't ensue.

◆ **Conduct Dry Runs.** You may have run over the new school carpool plan or discussed how you won't be home in the afternoons anymore a dozen times in conversation with your ten-year-old son, but saying and doing are two different things. He may still be unsettled when the actual day comes that those changes take place. So ease into it. Run through a few trial sessions before your new job starts by spending time away from the house all day one weekend so he gets a sense of what it will be like when you're away at work.

◆ **Lighten Your Load.** No point in stressing yourself out unnecessarily in this time of change. If you have to let a few things slide here and there—leaving a few unwashed dishes in the sink overnight or being fifteen minutes late to your child's soccer game—let it go. The same holds true at work if you have to leave work early for family. Just remember, there are going to be compromises on both sides along the way.

◆ **Make Time for One Another.** With schedules changing, stress levels fluctuating, and perhaps a certain level of tension running through a household, at least initially it's important to make time on the weekends, at night, or whenever a family can get together to simply enjoy one another without worrying about who's doing what chore now that things have changed.

Chapter 8

Mastering Networking

If you think the best time to network is in the throes of a job search, you've already lost out on an abundance of new work opportunities. The ideal time to explore your network of professional contacts is when you're currently employed. It is as important to maintain connections with people when you don't need their help as it is when you do. Let networking contacts dry up because you currently have a job and you can count on them not being available or having forgotten about you by the time you really need their assistance.

The problem, for most people anyway, is that they rarely squeeze in time in their busy schedules to maintain professional contacts that do not play a role in their everyday business dealings. That's a huge mistake. And remaining on your contact people's radar is quickly and easily done if you make it a regular practice. It doesn't have to be a lengthy dinner or even a phone call. An occasional e-mail can do the trick; or try sending an article related to your profession now and then to colleagues to keep communication fresh enough so that it's not awkward when you finally do reach out the next time you're looking for work. Doing so will pay off immeasurably when you want a new job or do really need to quickly tap a wide network of contacts.

For a lot of people, networking is more horrifying than root canals or public speaking. That is as true for older workers as it is for college students trying to land their first job. "I've been flabbergasted at how much worse at networking older workers have gotten in the past few years," says Dr. Randall Hansen of job site Quintessential Careers. "And the biggest excuses I hear are so lame. Their excuses are usually along the lines of, 'Well, most of my network is my age or older and they are all retired, so they're of no value.'" That rings hollow to Hansen. "My response is, just because they're retired doesn't mean they're not valuable. Plus there are a lot of organizations that have alumni clubs for people retired." There are also plenty of other organizations—many of them free—that older workers can take advantage of. "And then my second response is to say, 'Go out and get some new people in your network.'"

Hansen has a point. In fact, when you break it down, **networking is really no more than casual conversations with multiple people.** They're simply focused on more specific topics than what you might ramble through during cocktail hour.

The truth is, networking can occur anywhere, anytime—it doesn't have to take the laborious, horrifying form of an industry trade-show schmoozefest. Certainly there's value in working a crowded room of industry executives. But if that's an alarming scenario to you because your style is more quiet and subtle, there are plenty of ways to learn about jobs, a new industry, or a particular profession without slapping on a nametag and doing the proverbial meet-and-greet.

More to the point, networking (let's call it comfortable, casual conversation) can be inspiring, uplift you, and help you generate ideas for a new job or even career. Networking opportunities can pop up anywhere—with old classmates, at your child's weekly soccer game, at the annual college alumni gathering, even in health clubs. Sharai Rudolphi, who was a stay-at-home mom for years, got her first break reentering the job market at her local gym. Shortly after returning to school to study human services, Rudolphi joined a nearby club. "I was there two days and they said, 'Would you like a job?' I worked one-on-one doing assessments with women looking to join the club. It honed my skills working individually with women"—a move that helped her build connections to earn a volunteer practicum at a local women's shelter working with abused families, which ultimately landed her a full-time job at the same agency.

Keys to Successful Networking

You never know when your networking efforts will pay off—you can find job leads in the least likely places and nothing but dead-end leads among groups that you thought would surely be interview-getting bonanzas. One of the biggest keys to networking—besides an immense energy level and the commitment to never give up—is to be as creative as possible. ExecuNet's CEO and founder Dave Opton recalls one particularly innovative networker looking for a job in financial services who decided he was frustrated with his job search and that it was time to get creative. He realized that to score a job lead, he would most likely have to touch an emotional chord with someone. So he looked for common ground he might have with professional contacts. With that in mind, he crafted a concise, one-page marketing letter (sans résumé) and sent it to each member of the board of trustees at his undergraduate college. Emphasizing their common educational connection and what surely was a shared goal they all had—to see the school's graduates succeed professionally—this job seeker explained in quick, clear terms his past work experience, that he was a financial executive in the midst of a career transition, and that he was hoping to become a CFO. He detailed the size company he was interested in, the salary he was willing to accept, and the fact that relocation was not an issue for him. Then he casually but graciously mentioned that he would be very interested to hear of any companies the trustees may know of in need of a senior financial executive. "Lo and behold, one of those board members was sitting on the board of a company in Florida that was in the range the applicant was interested in. The board member sent the letter to the company's CEO and said, 'You might want to talk to this job seeker,'" Opton says. "He got the job."

That's extraordinarily clever personal marketing, to be sure. But such links to job leads exist in almost everyone's life—you just need to take some time to think about where and with whom. Board members are a particularly worthwhile group to tap, because they rarely sit on only one board, which makes them great resources for lots of other corporate contacts.

A Painful Process?

There's no getting around it: Conducting a job search is a deeply personal, ego-bashing endeavor. There's little in the world more wounding than a series of rejections that is all too easy to interpret as a supreme lack of faith in your skills and abilities on the part of corporate America. But research shows that people get hired for a host of reasons—personality, appearance, the mood of the interviewer, being the last applicant (and therefore most easily remembered), and other reasons that can have little if anything to do with actual abilities.

But regardless of how and why the hiring decision is finally made, it takes getting in the door first, which, job-search consultants widely agree, is most often accomplished through effective networking. **Experts note that anywhere from 70 to 80 percent of all job offers result from a networking contact.** That means your networking skills need to be sharp. One of the best ways to do that, Opton says, is to depersonalize your job search and networking efforts. Sound impossible? Think of your job search as a sales process, but this time the product is you. "Examine yourself at ten thousand feet," so to speak, advises Opton. What features about you would convince a potential "buyer" that you are the best person for the job? Sounds silly, but the tactic helps job seekers focus on their specific characteristics and talents and helps alleviate stress by deemphasizing the personal pain that accompanies so many employment searches.

A few additional networking hints to consider:

◆ **Don't Lose Touch.** The best and easiest way to build professional networking contacts may be to remain in touch with people you've worked with in the past—former colleagues, clients, counterparts at other firms. Even if you left the industry a long time ago, these folks may know of openings or key industry hotpoints that could help you land a job years later.

◆ **Make Contacts Work for You.** Not literally, of course, but don't get someone's business card, call them, and then assume their usefulness is over if they don't have a hot job lead for you. After you've developed a rapport, ask them who else they may know within your industry or profession. And maintain regular contact with them over a period of time. The same holds true for expanding contacts among former co-workers, association contacts, even friends and family.

◆ **Tap Industry Resources.** Want to write ad copy but have no ad agency contacts? Start attending advertising industry events. The American Association of Advertising Agencies, for example, has twenty-five regional councils nationwide with forums and opportunities to learn about advertising. The same holds true for virtually every industry in business today—as evidenced by the tens of thousands of organizations in the United States.

◆ **Walk in the Front Door.** One of the best ways to make contacts within an industry is to meet face to face with key contacts through informational interviews. It's an age-old tactic every overeager college grad has tried at some point. But it's not limited to any particular age group. The key: Be prepared when someone agrees to meet with you. Make sure to leave an impression that you've done your industry homework, but leave plenty of room for them to talk—people love to be advisers.

◆ **Volunteer.** Want to move from marketing pharmaceutical products to organizing events at your regional concert hall? Volunteer your services at theaters, dance halls, concert spaces, places that will help you meet people in the industry. And make yourself known—quietly ushering people to their seats during shows or working in the theater office and conscientiously, but silently, mailing out promo pieces may not get you noticed unless there happens to be a keenly observant supervisor running the show. Instead, verbalize your ideas—at the right time, of course—and offer to work on tasks above and beyond your required role.

♦ **Always Be Networking.** The contact for the job of a lifetime could be standing next to you at a beachside hot dog stand. Be open to meeting new people and striking up conversations about work anywhere and everywhere you go.

Finding Your Ideal Network

Of course, to network effectively you have to be relaxed with whomever you're talking to. And that means feeling at home in your networking environment. Whether it's a professional organization, industry trade show, local church meeting, even your monthly book group, it's important to find a group of people whom you feel comfortable bouncing ideas and questions off and seeking advice from. It's also crucial that you have a significant interest in the group you're joining. If you think attending the local marketing association's meetings might garner some hot leads for sales jobs, but you find the meetings painfully dull, there's a good chance your networking effort will flop. "Join a group because it is of interest to you, not because you think it's going to be the networking panacea of the universe," says Opton. You're much more likely to engage people and have them connect with you if you're discussing a topic in a group you both find interesting.

Can't find a networking group that fits your needs? Create your own. Plenty of laid-off midlevel managers, for example, have started their own weekly breakfast networking groups by inviting two friends to participate, then asking them to in turn invite their friends or colleagues. Keep the group small. Limiting membership to a dozen or two well-known friends and colleagues can help maintain a level of intimacy and trust among group members and increase chances for greater sharing of advice, hot job leads, and other valuable information.

If you feel you may need a shove when it comes to networking, joining groups that focus on and encourage peer contacts through structured networking activities may be a huge help in getting started. Groups like ExecuNet, which caters to managers and executives who typically make six figures or more a year, offer very structured networking activities in their meetings. Similar groups offer weekly meetings where job seekers can network face to face with others in search of employment. That's key, according to Opton. Even in the best of networking situations, it takes time to create a relaxed environment, level of comfort, and trust enough among members to share job leads or business contacts.

Something for job seekers to keep in mind: Networking is one of the most effective methods to landing a job (some 70 percent of ExecuNet's members find work that way), but it doesn't happen after one meeting. Patience is key. "Some say it takes six to eight contacts with someone before you feel enough of a rapport to share things other than recommending a dry cleaner," Opton says.

In a market where job seekers can be out of work for months at a time, giving out contacts is done with great caution. "But that doesn't mean that, for example, someone won't give you information about a job posting or the name of a recruiter," Opton says. After all, trust is established through informational exchanges.

Quick Networking Dos and Don'ts

When looking for a job, networking faux pas are almost as important as networking strategies. Practice these surefire tips, and avoid these all-too-common mistakes:

Networking Dos

♦ **Tell the World.** You should tell everyone and anyone that you're looking for work, and don't be afraid to dredge up any old contacts—you never know where they may lead.

♦ **Ask for Referrals.** Whether in an informational interview or contacting your best friend's boss, everyone you meet represents an additional contact for your job search. Don't be afraid to ask for a referral to people they know if you feel you've established a good rapport.

♦ **Explore All Resources.** Landing a job is a numbers game as much as anything else. Do nothing but peruse the Sunday want ads and you'll seriously limit your chances of landing work. Instead, reach out to every contact you have, go to association or professional meetings for your industry, attend alumni meetings, church, or trade shows—whatever it takes to find leads for work.

♦ **Don't Go in Blind.** Got an informational interview with a hot firm? Treat it like a real job interview—it could turn into one on the spot. Also, if you look ill prepared, your chances of gaining referral contacts from that person will be shot. Check out the company's Web site at a bare minimum, and read up on the industry in trade publications and other media outlets if you can.

♦ **Create an Elevator Pitch.** You can't network effectively if you can't articulate what it is you do currently or are hoping to do. The best way to do that is to craft a thirty-second pitch (long enough to include your goals and skills, but short enough to be said during the course of an elevator ride) that you can rattle off at conferences, in networking meetings, in informational interviews, and other places. You don't want the pitch to be stiff or forced, however, so practice—a lot—in front of a mirror or with a friend.

♦ **Follow Up.** Just as with job interviews, it pays to send thank-you notes and follow-up correspondence after informational interviews or even with fellow job seekers who provide hot job leads. And it's one more way to get your name in front of the right people.

♦ **Take Initiative.** Don't sit back after a few initial phone calls or informational interviews and expect people to follow up with you. Most people are so busy that even if they were favorably impressed by you when you first met, they may not have the time to reach out to you again. If you're worried about being intrusive, drop them an e-mail rather than phoning.

Networking Don'ts

♦ **Don't Burn Bridges.** Seems like common sense, but in their desperation to land a job or snag a new contact, many people will overstep their bounds and abuse their networking relationships. If, for example, someone in your networking group gives you the name of a key executive but asks that you don't mention her name, be respectful of that.

♦ **Never Ask for a Job.** Plenty of jobs have been landed during interviews that were supposed to be just informational but evolved when an employer was particularly impressed with a job seeker. And all applicants hope the same will happen to them. But odds are it won't, and if you ask for a job you're sure to put off your contact.

♦ **Don't Lie.** Or even stretch the truth. If someone gives you a contact based on a misrepresentation of your abilities or job history, you might tarnish your reputation. And you'll likely be doing a disservice to yourself by landing contacts for positions you aren't really qualified to fill.

◆ **Don't Be Vague.** This goes back to formulating an elevator pitch. Make sure you have a clear, precise vision of what kind of job or at least what area of an industry you're looking to find work in. Besides the fact that people probably won't provide job leads or contacts if they don't know what it is you're looking for, they probably don't want their precious contacts to associate them with such an unfocused job seeker.

Overcoming Networking Hurdles

Dreading that seemingly disingenuous or energy-zapping, hour-long networking session? There are ways to ease the pain. Try these tactics if schmoozing sends you into a frenzy.

◆ **Bring a Buddy.** For a lot of people, networking is as appealing as the annual trek to the doctor for a physical. If the thought of hobnobbing with strangers makes you physically ill with unease, lighten the load by bringing a fellow job seeker or a friend. That way you always have someone there for moral support; in addition, conversations are sometimes easier to start when you're not alone. Just remember, don't let your companion's presence prevent you from networking—after all, that's the whole reason you're there. Prepare cue words, if necessary, to indicate when you need your buddy to walk away while you pursue some more in-depth job information with your current networking contact.

◆ **Practice, Practice, Practice.** Preparation is the key to success with anything. And that involves lots of practice. Practice pitches in front of mirrors, think of questions you can ask or may be asked during informational interviews, even practice something as simple as a handshake and introduction for a networking meeting if need be. **If you're not prepared, you might as well stay home.**

◆ **Find a Comfort Zone.** If a group that you've joined isn't panning out, find another that's more your style or speed. Some people can network every night until they're blue in the face. If you're a true introvert and a room full of people just zaps your energy, don't force yourself to succumb to that kind of anxiety night after night. You won't be in any shape to make an impression and win people's confidence. Find a level of networking that's comfortable enough for you to stick with.

◆ **Think of It as a Conversation.** Part of the stress of networking is that people walk into an association meeting or networking conference and immediately feel they have to perform. That's way too stressful an approach. Try to relax and think of the experience as you would a cocktail party or informal business gathering over lunch. If it helps, don't jump in with career credentials or your polished elevator pitch. Start things off casually with a general conversation—about sports, where someone's from, or whatever it takes to break the ice.

Resources for Networkers

If you're more likely to join an existing networking group than create your own, you might consider checking out some of the following organizations:

◆ **The Transition Network,** www.thetransitionnetwork.com. Launched in New York City in 2000 with a heavy emphasis still in that geographic area, the networking group's founder, Christine Millen, has managed to expand the organization nationwide with chapters in other major cities, such as Washington, DC, San Francisco, and Chicago. The network offers an opportunity for women only to network with peers and examine other possibilities for their next phase of life. Millen stresses that the organization is not a support group, but a place that offers discussion and activities to figure out the next stage in life. The Transition Network's membership base consists of 358 people along with 1,000 newsletter subscribers. Membership costs seventy-five dollars a year, but the monthly newsletter is free and available online, and nonmembers can pay twenty-five dollars to visit a chapter meeting to see if they're interested in joining.

◆ **America's Career InfoNet,** www.acinet.org. Probably the most comprehensive job-search Web site available, InfoNet is less a straight networking tool than a vast resource of invaluable information about companies, jobs by state, and more. It even includes details about over five thousand scholarships for those thinking of going back to school.

◆ **Execunet,** www.execunet.com. If you're a mid- to upper-level manager who makes more than a hundred thousand dollars a year, you'll find strong networking possibilities in this organization. Meetings aren't limited to those who pull in over six figures, but this is definitely not a group for lower-level managers. It's a rich resource of people—both employed and unemployed—who maintain a healthy interest in expanding their business contacts for job leads. The sixteen-year-old organization says it's helped more than 150,000 executives advance. But it does come at a price. Membership packages start at $150 for three months. Typical meetings involve a brief networking session, discussion of a key job-search or business topic, and plenty of time to practice your elevator pitch on others.

◆ **Financial Executives Networking Group,** www.thefeng.org. An international organization of twenty thousand members, FENG was started in 1991 by Donald Gonsalves, a financial executive who was over fifty and felt a networking resource for his age group and skill set was lacking. The group is largely intended for networking among financial executives, although others—marketing managers, for example—have been known to frequent meetings. Very helpful, hard-and-fast networking is the name of the game here: Newcomers are expected to bring nametags, résumés and business cards, and a ninety-second elevator pitch to their first meeting. Membership is free.

◆ **Five O'Clock Club,** www.fiveoclockclub.com. Perhaps one of the country's oldest networking groups, the Five O'Clock Club was formed in Philadelphia in 1883. A forty-nine-dollar membership fee gives you access to weekly job-search strategy groups that, with the exception of members at physical sites in New York, Washington, DC, and Chicago, meet via teleconferencing in small groups of four to six people, grouped by salary level. Organization leaders claim that, on average, networkers snag job offers within ten sessions. But the key, they insist, is regular attendance at every Monday-night teleconference.

◆ **Wall Street Journal Career Journal,** www.careerjournal.com/ calendar/. Can't find the right networking group in your area? Check out the calendar listings available on the *Wall Street Journal*'s Web site in the career journal section. The link above offers a search tool for local networking groups and meetings by state.

If you still have trouble finding an appropriate networking group for your job-search needs, you can always try contacting your local chamber of commerce, library, college, or labor office.

A Word on Mass Mailings

Like many of life's endeavors, landing a job is largely a numbers game. The more networking groups you join, the more meetings you attend, the more people you meet, the more contacts you get, and the more résumés you send out, the more interviews you'll land. All of which brings you one step closer to that coveted offer. But the numbers game can get the best of some job seekers.

When one Boston-area marketing executive was laid off, he contemplated sending out thousands of résumés through a service that supplies a database of corporate contacts in your profession for a fee—which can run as high as two dollars a letter. Send out fifteen hundred letters, which is not atypical, and suddenly the cost of your job search just skyrocketed.

Direct mail can be an effective way to reach job contacts at various companies, and sending out thousands of pieces is certainly committing to the numbers theory—the one that says, *Hit enough places and eventually something will stick.* There's some truth in it, but there's also the danger of whittling away funds that you should spend carefully as you network and look for a job. And it can be a frivolous expenditure, given the preponderance of low-cost or free networking groups and the low rate of return on such efforts. "You're really rolling the dice big time," says Opton. "If you can afford to do that, it may be a tool to use, but in the best-case scenario you'll get a direct-mail response rate. Those usually run less than 1 percent."

But if that 1 percent lands you a job it was worth it, right? There are plenty of people—direct-mail companies certainly among them—who would argue that even if you spend ten thousand dollars blasting your résumé to hundreds of companies nationwide, if it gets you a senior-level job a month faster than you would have through traditional job-hunting methods, the mailing just paid for itself. But there's always the chance your response rate will be zero—or that, even at 1 or 2 percent, it still won't yield a job offer.

Probably a better approach—and certainly cheaper—is to research a few dozen companies yourself where you'd like to work, then find key contacts there and send your résumé to them directly. Networking again may come in handy here—you never know when a colleague at a local meeting may know the head of HR or finance at one of the companies you're targeting. It happens all the time.

Chapter 9

Retirement Hurdles Lead to Work

Like every other social norm, retirement has changed as we've evolved as a society, in industry, and, most recently, in the area of technology. Up to the early twentieth century, Americans largely lived and worked on farms, and families took care of each other—which meant that older Americans could count on the next generation's laborers supporting them later in life (although most worked far into old age). Of course, as the industrial revolution swept the country, that dynamic changed.

Issues of aging and how to care for older Americans were being debated at least as far back as the early twentieth century. In her book *The Evolution of Retirement: An American Economic History, 1880–1990* (part of the National Bureau of Economic Research Series on Long-Term Factors in Economic Development), Dora L. Costa, an economics professor at the Massachusetts Institute of Technology, writes that the Committee on Economic Security under President Franklin Roosevelt considered older workers to be more or less incapable of working to support themselves. Costa writes, "the committee believed that . . . modern industry had no need for older workers and, other than their labor, these workers had no other means with which to support themselves."

The American workplace has come a long way since then, and so have older workers' expectations of their lifestyles, financial stability, and life expectancies, as well as their vision of how their retirement and later work years should pan out. For starters, those years are substantially longer now than in the early 1900s, when people were happy to have just a few years to live at the end of their lives without working. Projected life expectancies for Americans have risen from forty-nine years in 1900 to seventy-six in 2000, according to the Federal Interagency Forum on Aging-Related Statistics. And that even sounds young by today's standards, given that medicine is helping so many people to live well into their eighties and beyond. **By 2050, the number of Americans over sixty-five is projected to reach eighty-two million.** That's an estimated 20 percent of the population that will be trying to fill their golden years. And given volatile markets and economies, plenty of corporate layoffs, declining investment funds, and unexpected costs in living, today more than ever older workers are seeking to fill those years with work.

A 2001 Harris Interactive poll found that new visions of what retirement can be are emerging among older Americans. The respondents to that poll were broken down into "ageless explorers," those who approach retirement with youthful enthusiasm and want to avoid boredom and strike up new interests; "comfortably contents," people who want a traditional, leisure-filled, travel-based retirement; "live for todays," who are eager to be active and adventurous but worry that their portfolios may hold them back; and "sick and tireds," individuals who aren't optimistic about their futures and haven't saved much over the years.

AGING THROUGH THE DECADES

Rise and Projected Rise in Population of Older Americans in the Twentieth and Twenty-First Centuries

Year	Number of Americans Over 65	Percentage of the Population
1900	3.1 million	4.1 percent
1910	4.0 million	4.3 percent
1920	4.9 million	4.7 percent
1930	6.6 million	5.4 percent
1940	9.0 million	6.9 percent
1950	12.3 million	8.2 percent
1960	16.6 million	9.2 percent
1970	20.1 million	9.9 percent
1980	25.5 million	11.3 percent
1990	31.2 million	12.6 percent
2000	35.0 million	12.4 percent
2010	39.7 million	13.2 percent
2020	53.7 million	16.5 percent
2030	70.3 million	20.0 percent
2040	77.2 million	20.5 percent
2050	82.0 million	20.3 percent

Source: Department of Health and Human Resources, Federal Interagency Forum on Aging-Related Statistics.

Many older workers nearing retirement, like Michael Dowhan, can become frustrated with their absence from the work world simply because they underestimated the costs of living without a full-time job. Dowhan has had a lesson in all those costs, from financial to personal. After he left a twenty-three-year professional career at age fifty-five, it took one month for Dowhan to realize that while he wanted less responsibility, he also missed the office atmosphere, and he needed more money, in part to pay for health benefits that he estimated would cost upward of four hundred dollars a month.

A former vice president at Deutsche Bank and a facilities manager at Cartier, he now works thirty-two hours a week at Barnes & Noble, and earns $250 for doing so. He admits the pay isn't on the level of his former jobs, but it covers his expenses and brings his medical premiums down to less than twenty dollars a week. The position also gives him the benefits of co-worker interaction and intellectual stimulation in an environment where he is surrounded by books.

His job, like many post-career positions with less responsibility and hours, offers Dowhan more appealing work hours, with a four-day workweek and three-day weekends. "I don't have a plan for exiting. There's no magic number where I'm saying, 'When I hit sixty-five or seventy, I'm leaving.' I'm going to work as long as I can."

Like many older workers, he has discovered that part-time work is ideal—it gives him his needed dose of workplace camaraderie and socialization and enough mental stimulation to prevent boredom. "There's no point in stepping out of the workforce," he says. "I did that for a month and said, 'Here it is the middle of the month and everyone has something to do or someplace to be. The weekends have no meaning.'"

And while Dowhan loves the intellectual and social interaction he's found now, he's also happy with his current responsibilities. He's been offered managerial positions at Barnes & Noble. His response: Thanks, but no thanks. "I'm fifty-nine, and I've paid my dues management-wise."

Retirement Considerations

Most people don't psychoanalyze their move into retirement. And that's okay, but the truth is that retirement is as much a psychological endeavor as it is a financial one. Are you prepared? Have you fully thought about how leaving the workplace you've been part of for the last decade or more might affect you emotionally? You might want to ask yourself if you've considered the following:

◆ Are you okay with letting go of a daily routine and structure? How will the sudden absence of projects, responsibilities, and mental challenges impact your daily intellectual needs?

◆ Have you put together a list of activities in your first few weeks out of the office that could keep you occupied and ease your transition into a life of not working?

◆ Have you considered what the structure of your day will be like outside work?

◆ How difficult will it be to walk away from the social network in your office? Have you thought about ways to replace that part of your life—through community activities, volunteering opportunities, part-time work, or a new career?

◆ Are there interests or hobbies you would like to explore with more intensity after you leave your job?

◆ Have you explored the possibility of coming back to your current employer on a part-time, full-time, or contractual freelance basis if not working becomes a decision you regret making?

◆ Have you talked to your family about how leaving work will affect you psychologically or emotionally? Have you discussed how retirement might change your daily routine with your spouse and other family members?

Getting Ahead

Dowhan isn't alone in wanting to maintain some level of work after a full-time career. For a large portion of older Americans, money struggles are a harsh reality. Such financial burdens are forcing myriad older workers to put off retirement, often to as late as seventy, according to an AARP study released in 2004. The choice seems to be: Work longer or live poorer.

People are choosing the former, and understandably so, says Drew Denning, director of retirement and investor services in Des Moines, Iowa, for the Principal Financial Group. "Our stats show for a couple retiring at sixty-five, there's a 38 percent chance that one will still be alive in thirty years and an 18 percent chance that one spouse will make it to one hundred. People underestimate their life expectancy." And financial planners don't always help. Denning continues: "There are a number of planning tools that perpetuate [the problem of financial instability in retirement] because the plans default to a twenty-year retirement."

More than half of nonretired Americans have saved less than ten thousand dollars for retirement, according to a January 2004 survey by Thrivent Financial, a nonprofit financial services company in Minneapolis. And it gets worse: A whopping 36 percent of the thousand respondents surveyed over the age of eighteen hadn't saved a penny.

Retirement, Shmetirement

One way to deal with a lack of retirement planning, of course, is to postpone retirement. A 2003 survey from AARP revealed that 45 percent of pre-retirees between fifty and seventy planned to work into

RETIREMENT SAVINGS AMONG AMERICANS

Amount Saved	Percentage of Population
$10,000–49,999	17 percent
$50,000–99,999	9 percent
$100,000–249,999	6 percent
$250,000–499,999	2 percent
$500,000–999,999	1 percent
$1 million or more	1 percent

Source: Thrivent Financial, 2003. Reprinted with permission.

their seventies or beyond—some because they had to, others out of a desire to remain employed. Indeed, a survey in late 2003 by the outplacement consulting firm Challenger, Gray & Christmas concluded that the fastest-growing segment of the U.S. labor market was workers fifty-five and older. The latest numbers from the Bureau of Labor Statistics put workers over fifty at just over 35.7 million.

Some companies are becoming sensitive to this phenomenon and stepping in with programs that can help workers who want to remain on staff longer than expected:

♦ Volkswagen of America Inc. offers an elder care flexible spending program that allows employees to allocate five thousand in pretax earnings into an account.

♦ St. Mary's Medical Center in Huntington, West Virginia, provides free breast cancer, skin cancer, and cervical exams to female employees and free annual checkups to all staff.

♦ SSM Health Care in St. Louis, Missouri, allows employees to work part time while collecting full retirement benefits.

♦ Intel has established a phased-retirement program so that employees can exit the company in stages and not retire all at once.

Drops in Social Security returns will only make matters bleaker. "Too many people feel that Social Security is half their retirement income," says Gary Chard, a financial adviser. "In reality it's probably more like 15 percent. It's certainly not something you can fall back on."

If you're hitting fifty and your retirement fund seems paltry, start reviewing it—don't give up hope and think that Social Security is your only saving grace or that you'll simply have to work your fingers to the bone until the day you die. It may seem pointless to start saving now, but the good news is that most older workers are making more than when they were thirty-five, so they can afford to put away five thousand dollars or more extra a year that they couldn't when they were younger. And a lot of people, faced with a smaller nest egg than they had hoped for as they move into their retirement years, realize they can tighten their belts, drop their cost of living a notch, and still maintain an enjoyable quality of life. You'd be surprised, also, at how many discretionary expenses you have each month— from that pedicure every other week to those extra shopping sprees, even that morning cup of Starbucks coffee that quickly add up and can be eliminated or purchased less often, saving hundreds of dollars a month. Review your expenses and you might be shocked to find as much as three thousand dollars in discretionary spending that you can eliminate each month. Invested properly, that can significantly boost a nest egg in no time. A good place to start is by asking questions like the following:

- How much income do you need to adequately live each year?
- Where are other areas you could cut expenses and save more money?
- Are your investments diversified into risk-appropriate funds?
- Should you start looking at part-time employment as an option to increase your income or improve your quality of life?
- Do you foresee any medical expenses you may have down the road? Are such health costs adequately covered?
- On a similar note, might you have any expected (or unexpected) fun expenses—weddings, anniversary parties, or other events—down the road that may be substantial cash drains when they arrive?
- How do you plan to expand your yearly activities upon retirement? Do you plan to travel more? Will you want to take classes? Do you plan on joining any clubs? Are there grandchildren you'll want to buy gifts for or fly in to visit you?

Managing your retirement fund is not unlike managing your own personal payroll system, Chard says—and that's exactly how people should think of it. Being disciplined about not spending extravagantly, paying yourself first and then your expenses each month, watching how much you dip into long-term savings, and being realistic about the annual withdrawal rate you can expect from your portfolio are all vital steps to making your retirement portfolio last.

Tapping the Financial-Planning Experts

If you're already behind in your retirement planning, you need help—fast. There are still plenty of savings options and ways to enjoy a fruitful retirement, even for those over fifty who may have lost much of their portfolio in recent years. Finding the right person or resource to put you back on target is invaluable. A solid financial planner can easily return you to the right track, but they can be pricey—many start at $150 an hour and go up from there. Also remember that some "advisers" are little more than brokers who simply want to cash in on commissions they generate from your moderately performing portfolio.

If a financial adviser is key to your portfolio rebound, here are a few tips to keep in mind:

♦ **Ask Around.** If you think you need a financial planner, one of the best ways to find one is by word of mouth. Ask your neighbors, friends, co-workers—anyone whose opinion you trust—for names of planners they've worked with. But don't assume their references are rock-solid, either. Ask planners themselves for at least five referrals of former or current clients, and additional referrals from those customers if they know of any.

♦ **Check Credentials.** The world's best financial adviser could have a degree in history, but be really savvy with investments. Likewise, a planner with multiple accounting degrees could come up short in advice regarding life insurance or other personal finance issues. That said, certifications can be a comfort in verifying that a financial adviser has acquired at least some level of experience in personal finance. A few to note: CFPs or certified financial planners have worked for at least three years in the field and have taken exams on financial planning. ChFCs or chartered financial consultants have studied and passed exams on personal finance at the American College in Bryn Mawr, Pennsylvania, a school sponsored by the insurance industry. CLUs or chartered life underwriters have taken courses in life insurance planning, but not necessarily personal finance or investment. RIAs or registered investment advisers have registered with the SEC as investment advisers. CFAs or chartered financial analysts are awarded designations by the Institute of Chartered Financial Analysts for completion of a series of exams in everything from economics to security analysis. Again, however, don't place all your confidence in these designations—check references and get feedback from former clients.

◆ **Do a Background Check.** If nothing else, you should at least check to see if a complaint has ever been made with the local Better Business Bureau—or, worse, your state securities office—against a planner you're considering using. If there has, obviously, walk away. There are hundreds of other planners out there.

◆ **Ask for a Plan Upfront.** There's perhaps no better way to gauge the viability of advisers than to actually see the plan of attack they have in mind to set your finances right. So ask to see proposals—not just for you, but also those prepared for former clients (names and vital information blacked out, of course). And be sure to ask financial planners what their investment strategy is overall.

◆ **Ask How Your Adviser Gets Paid.** This is key. It's wise to hire a planner who simply charges a flat fee for services, rather than one who gets paid on commission. The reason? Those seeking commissions may be tempted to increase the number of transactions within your portfolio to pull in more money. This can, and probably will, put their personal gain above your best interests as an investor.

Now that you've got a financial adviser, you should know what to expect from him and how best to work with him. For starters, make sure the relationship is one where you meet on a regular basis—something that will be as much up to you as your financial planner. It's probably smart to get together at least once a year once your plan is up and running, but meeting monthly, or even weekly, when you're just starting to formulate your plan and figure out all of your financial options is a wise move. Get ready for a barrage of questions, financial work-sheets, and other materials that will give your adviser a better picture of your financial situation, where you plan to go, and how to get you there.

A good adviser will not only help you sort through potential investment plans and products you can look into to boost your portfolio, but also make a detailed examination of your lifestyle, spending habits, financial values, and more. That said, don't ignore your own gut instincts by assuming that your adviser is the ultimate, all-knowing financial sage. If you think her advice isn't right in a particular matter, speak up. Remember also that even the best financial planner can't work miracles. There's only so much she can do for someone who, for example, is fifty, hasn't saved a dime, and is pinned down under enormous debt. She can certainly help you with such issues—depending, of course, on your initial financial standing.

Do-It-Yourself Financial Planning

If you don't have the cash to plunk down for advice on how to make more money, and, if you're willing to go the route of self-education, seemingly endless arrays of Web sites offer free information about retirement planning, using retirement calculators, stock performance, wise investment decisions, and more. Indeed, they have become the new best friends of many older Americans scrambling to become more financially savvy in the aftermath of seeing their portfolios ravaged in the stock market. It's probably wise to formulate a plan off a few key sites that you find are best oriented to your goals and needs, and you find easy to navigate and understand. Pulling all your information from one site—even if the advice is sound and credible—may not be so wise. One other note to keep in mind: A few of these sites, which once offered free information, are now asking for fees, but those that do usually only require a nominal charge.

Financial-Planning Web Resources

Type "retirement planning" into Google and the search engine brings up more than two million results. There's certainly no shortage of information out there! Of course, if you're late in planning for retirement, the last thing you want to do is parse through two million Web pages. Here are a few solid sites to get you started:

◆ **Money magazine,** www.money.cnn.com. The magazine's joint Web site with CNN offers robust, practical, hard-hitting information on retirement and investing—plenty of it geared for novices. A great place to find fast answers.

♦ **About.com,** www.about.com. This stands out as one of the most practical, thorough Web sites for finding how-to articles on nearly any subject, including, of course, retirement and investment planning—and even tips on working, changing careers, and other ideas for older workers.

♦ **American Association of Retired Persons,** www.aarp.org. AARP's household-name status exists for good reason. The group's site offers an immense amount of information on retirement financial planning, from selecting an IRA to the nuances of annuities.

♦ **The Motley Fool,** www.fool.com. Long a respected financial Web site despite its name, the Motley Fool offers (among many other tools) a basic introduction that breaks down retirement almost back to front, looking at your perceived figure lifestyle and helping you work backward from there to get it.

♦ **Department of Labor,** www.dol.gov. Government Web sites are notorious for reams of pages that can be clunky and difficult to wade through. Not so the DOL. For example, one online document, "10 Ways to Beat the Clock and Prepare for Retirement," provides no-frills points that all workers should be thinking about as they invest for retirement. It also covers specific demographics, such as women and retirement.

♦ *Smart Money* **magazine,** www.smartmoney.com/retirement. The magazine about personal finance and owned by the *Wall Street Journal* is chock-full of free, useful online articles about retirement—everything from actual retirement worksheets to retirement rollovers and 401(k) planning.

♦ **The Alliance for Investor Education,** www.investoreducation.org. Perhaps one of the most comprehensive investment Web sites around, the AIE is dedicated to educating people about investments. With that in mind, the site offers solid, basic information, such as

"A Guide to Understanding Mutual Funds," similar guides to bonds, and an entire crucial section on avoiding various investment scams.

♦ **Kiplinger,** www.kiplinger.com. The eighty-year-old hallmark of personal finance delivers once again online with a ream of articles, retirement calculators, and investment and planning tools that are all backed up by decades of expertise.

♦ **Social Security Administration,** www.ssa.gov. Like its sister site, the Department of Labor, the Social Security Administration's Web site is an online bastion of vital tips, tools, and information straight from the horse's mouth.

♦ **Path To Investing,** www.siainvestor.com. This site, created by the nonprofit group Foundation for Investor Education, is dedicated to providing information to investors of all ages and experience. Esteemed guest writers from places like Freddie Mac, Wharton, and Yale offer tips on homeownership and asset allocation. The site is good for seasoned investors as well as newcomers with informational articles on topics as simple as finding money to invest.

♦ **Growing Wealthy,** www.growingwealthy.com. Not a place for original advice per se, this site provides a valuable service by compiling lists of books about personal finance and retirement, as well as links to purchase the material.

♦ **MPower,** www.mpower.com. Now owned by well-respected financial information service Morningstar, MPower provides articles, tips, and insight into the best personal investment choices.

Work Life After 50

The good news in all of this is that being handed that proverbial pink slip or finding yourself suddenly itching to get out of your current work situation later in life is not, by any means, the end of your professional world. There are endless arrays of work options out there for people over fifty—opportunities that are growing almost exponentially each year. The key is to get focused, know what you want, realize what it will take to get there, then deliberately, methodically work toward that goal— with a willingness to compromise along the way.

AARP's 2004 Best Employers for Workers Over 50

Adecco Employment Services, Melville, NY,
www.adeccousa.com
A staffing and human resource solutions company that
places temporary and full-time employees at client locations.

Beaumont Hospitals, Southfield, MI,
www.Beaumonthospitals.com
A provider of health care services, medical education, and
medical research.

Bon Secours Richmond Health System, Richmond, VA,
www.bonsecours.com
A not-for-profit, multifacility health care system with three
hospitals and more than twenty-four outpatient service sites.

Brethren Village, Lancaster, PA,
www.bv.org
A not-for-profit continuing care retirement community
offering choices and services to keep residents living
independently for as long as possible.

Centegra Health System, Woodstock, IL,
www.centegra.com
A health care system that includes several hospitals, the
Centegra Primary Care physician network, a fitness center,
and over twenty additional sites throughout its service area.

The Charles Stark Draper Laboratory, Inc., Cambridge, MA,
www.draper.com
A private, not-for-profit corporation engaged in applied
research, engineering development, technology transfer, and
advanced technical education.

Deere & Company, Moline, IL,
www.johndeere.com
Manufactures, distributes, and finances a broad range of
agricultural, construction, forestry, commercial, and
consumer equipment.

Delaware North Companies, Inc., Buffalo, NY,
www.delawarenorth.com
A hospitality and food service provider that provides visitor
services at national parks and attractions, resorts, and at
more than fifty sporting venues and thirty airports in the
United States.

DentaQuest Ventures, Inc., Boston, MA,
www.dentaquest.com
National administrator of dental benefits.

First Horizon National Corporation, Memphis, TN,
www.firsthorizon.com
A nationwide financial services institution providing services
to individuals and businesses.

Gemini, Incorporated, Cannon Falls, MN,
www.signletters.com
A manufacturer of metal and plastic letters for outdoor
signage and customized decorative metal plaques.

Hoffmann-La Roche, Inc., Nutley, NJ,
www.rocheusa.com
An innovation-driven health care company with core
businesses in pharmaceuticals and diagnostics.

Lee County Electric Cooperative, North Fort Myers, FL,
www.lcec.net
A not-for-profit electric distribution cooperative providing
service and energy products to 165,000 customers in
southwest Florida.

Lincoln Financial Group, Philadelphia, PA,
www.lfg.com
Provides financial and security products to individuals and
businesses.

Loudoun Healthcare, Inc., Leesburg, VA,
www.loudounhealthcare.org
A not-for-profit health care organization providing a full
continuum of quality health care services.

Minnesota Life, St. Paul, MN,
www.minnesotalife.com
Provides insurance, pension and investment products to
more than six million clients in all fifty states and Puerto
Rico.

Mitretek Systems, Falls Church, VA,
www.mitretek.org
A nonprofit research and engineering company.

New York University Medical Center, New York, NY,
www.med.nyu.edu
A not-for-profit health care organization comprising the
NYU Hospitals Center and the NYU School of Medicine.

North Memorial Health Care, Robbinsdale, MN,
www.northmemorial.com
A nonprofit health care provider with more than eight
hundred physicians and five thousand employees in its
system.

Pitney Bowes, Inc., Stamford, CT,
www.pitneybowes.com
A provider of integrated mail and document management
systems, services, and solutions.

Principal Financial Group, Des Moines, IA,
www.principal.com
Offers businesses, individuals, and institutional clients a wide
range of financial products and services.

Scottsdale Healthcare, Scottsdale, AZ,
www.shc.org
A nonprofit health care provider with two hospitals,
outpatient centers, home health services, and a wide range of
community outreach programs.

Scripps Health, San Diego, CA,

www.scrippshealth.org

A not-for-profit, community-based health care system that includes five acute and tertiary care hospitals, numerous outpatient facilities, and home health care services.

Smurfit-Stone Container Corporation, Clayton, MO,

www.smurfit-stone.com

A manufacturer of paperboard, paper-based packaging, and other packaging materials and paper-based products.

Sonoco, Hartsville, SC,

www.sonoco.com

A manufacturer of industrial and consumer packaging products and provider of packaging services.

SSM Health Care, St. Louis, MO,

www.ssmhc.com

A health care network sponsored by the Franciscan Sisters of Mary that delivers patient care in the St. Louis region.

St. Mary's Medical Center, Huntington, WV,

www.st-marys.org

A regional medical center in the tristate region of West Virginia, Ohio, and Kentucky, specializing in cardiac, oncology, trauma, and neuroscience services.

Stanley Consultants, Inc., Muscatine, IA,

www.stanleyconsultants.com

A multidisciplinary consulting firm that provides engineering, environmental, and construction services worldwide.

The Methodist Hospital, Houston, TX,
www.methodisthealth.com
A nonprofit health care organization made up of a flagship
hospital, The Methodist Hospital, and three community hospitals.

The Vanguard Group, Valley Forge, PA,
www.vanguard.com
An investment management company that provides an array
of financial products and services, including mutual fund
investments and employer-sponsored retirement plan
services.

Volkswagen of America, Inc., Auburn Hills, MI,
www.vw.com
Manufacturer of passenger cars and trucks.

WELBRO Building Corporation, Maitland, FL,
www.welbro.com
A full-service construction management and general
contracting company.

West Virginia University Hospitals, Morgantown, WV,
www.wvuh.com
A private, not-for-profit corporation that is closely tied to
West Virginia University and includes three hospitals, a
trauma center, and the WVU Eye Institute.

Westgate Resorts, Orlando, FL,
www.westgateresorts.com
A privately held time-share company that employs over five
thousand people throughout the country.

Zurich North America, Schaumburg, IL,

www.zurichna.com

A commercial property-casualty insurance provider serving the multinational, middle market, and small-business sectors in the United States and Canada.

Source: AARP, 2004 Best Employers for Workers Over 50. Reprinted with permission.

Appendix B

Additional Reading

Too Young to Retire: 101 Ways to Start the Rest of Your Life. Marika Stone and Howard Stone. Plume Books, 2004.

Going Back to Work: A Survival Guide for Comeback Moms. Mary W. Quigley and Loretta E. Kaufman. St. Martin's Press, 2004.

Don't Retire, Rewire! 5 Steps to Fulfilling Work That Fuels Your Passion, Suits Your Personality, or Fills Your Pocket. Jeri Sedlar and Rick Miners. Alpha Books, 2003.

What Do You Want to Do When You Grow Up? Starting the Next Chapter of Your Life. Dorothy Cantor. Little, Brown, 2002.

Challenges of the Third Age: Meaning and Purpose in Later Life. Robert S. Weiss and Scott A. Bass. Oxford University Press, 2001.

The Creative Age: Awakening Human Potential in the Second Half of Life. Gene D. Cohen. Perennial Currents, 2001.

Generations at Work: Managing the Clash of Veterans, Boomers, Xers, and Nexters in Your Workplace. Ron Zemke,

Claire Raines, and Bob Filipczak. American Management Association, 2000.

Age Power: How the 21st Century Will Be Ruled by the New Old. Ken Dychtwald. Jeremy P. Tarcher/Penguin, 2000.

ReFirement: A Boomer's Guide to Life After 50. James V. Gambone. Kirk House Publishers, 2000.

Older and Active: How Americans Over 55 Are Contributing to Society. Scott A. Bass. Yale University Press, 1995.

"Back to School at Age 50," *AARP The Magazine* (AARP magazine.org), www.aarpmagazine.org/lifestyle/Articles/a2003-10-14-backtoschool1.html, December 21, 2004.